The Enduring Presence of Christianity in Lebanon

Fadi P. Deek

Purple Breeze

PRESS

Purple Breeze Press, LLC

purplebreezepress.com
The Enduring Presence of Christianity in Lebanon
© 2025 Fadi P. Deek

Except in the case of brief quotations used in articles and reviews, no part of this book may be reproduced, stored in a retrieval system, or transmitted in any form without the author's permission.

Library of Congress Cataloguing in Publication Data
Names: Deek, Fadi P., author
Title: *The Enduring Presence of Christianity in Lebanon*
Description: First edition. | Purple Breeze Press, 2025

Library of Congress Control Number: 2025920389

ISBN Paperback: 979-8-9918895-5-1

Book designed by Streetlight Graphics

TABLE OF CONTENTS

Note to Readers ix
Introduction xiii
About the Book xvii
   Some Relevant Calendar Terminologies xix
Part One: From the Canaanites to the Maronites xxi
Chapter 1. The Rich Heritage of Ancient Lebanon 1
   Lebanon Through the Ages 3
   The Cultures and Religions of Lebanon in the Ancient World 7
Chapter 2. Lebanon in Biblical History 13
   Observations from the Old Testament 14
   Observations from the New Testament 18
   Early Christianity and the Spread of the Gospel in Lebanon 20
   Phoenician Thoughts and Christian Theology 23
Chapter 3. Christianity in Lebanon
under the Roman and Byzantine Empires 27
   The Roman Empire 28
   The Byzantine Empire 30
   Antioch 32
   Laying the Foundations at Beit Mārūn 33
   The Ecumenical Council of Chalcedon 34
Chapter 4. The Maronites 37
   Keeping and Growing the Faith 37

    A Bold Move—First Patriarch for the Maronites 40
    Maronite Transition from Antioch to Mount Lebanon—
    The Making of a New Homeland 43
Part Two: From the Arab Conquests to the Crusades 49
Chapter 5. The Arab Conquests and the Spread of Islam 51
    The Impact of Islam on the Byzantine Empire and Lebanon 52
    The Sunni-Shia Schism 54
    The Marada Resistance in Mount Lebanon 55
Chapter 6. Muslim Caliphates and Dynasties in Lebanon 59
    The Rashidun Caliphate 61
    The Umayyad Caliphate 63
    The Abbasid Caliphate 64
    The Fatimid Caliphate 69
    The Seljuks 70
    The Ayyubids 71
Chapter 7. The Great Christian Schism 75
    Context 76
    A Breaking Point 79
    The Schisms of the Early Church 81
Chapter 8. The Provoking Factors of the Schisms 85
    Geographic Factors 86
    Linguistic Factors 86
    Cultural Factors 86
    Political Factors 87
    Social Factors 87
    Theological Factors 88
    Persistent Divisions 90
Chapter 9. The New Denominations of Christianity 93
    The Antiochene Syriac Maronite Church 94
    The Greek Orthodox Church of Antioch 94
    The Greek Catholic Church of Antioch 95
    The Syriac Orthodox Church of Antioch 96

The Syriac Catholic Church of Antioch ... 97
  The Assyrian Church of the East ... 97
  The Chaldean Catholic Church ... 98
  The Armenian Apostolic Church ... 98
  The Armenian Catholic Church ... 99
  The Coptic Orthodox Church of Alexandria ... 99
  The Coptic Catholic Church ... 100
  Rapprochement and Reconciliation ... 100

Chapter 10. The Crusades ... 103
  Impact on Christians in Lebanon ... 104
  The First Crusade (1096-1099) ... 105
  The Second Crusade (1147-1149) ... 107
  The Third Crusade (1187-1192) ... 107
  The Fourth Crusade (1202-1204) ... 107
  The Final Crusades (1208-1291) ... 108
  Migration to Cyprus ... 109
  Ramifications of the End of the Crusades
  on the Lebanese Christians ... 110

Part Three: From the Mamluks to the Lebanese Diaspora ... 113

Chapter 11. The Return of the Caliphates
and Expanding Western Relations ... 115
  The Mamluks ... 116
  The Black Death ... 118
  Expanding Western Relations—
  Latinization and Cultural Renaissance ... 118

Chapter 12. The Ottoman Caliphate and Consequential
Occupation in Lebanon ... 123
  The Ottomans in Lebanon ... 124
  A Period of Expansion in the Christian
  Communities in Lebanon ... 127

Chapter 13. Christian-Druze Self-Rule in Mount Lebanon ... 131
  The Maans ... 131

The Chehabs ... 132
External Challenges—Egypt's Invasion ... 133
Internal Challenges—
The Changing Dynamics of Christian-Druze Relations ... 134
The 1840 Christian-Druze Conflict ... 135
The Qaim-Maqamate Provincial System (1843-1861) ... 136
The 1860 Christian-Druze Conflict ... 138
The Keserwan Revolt in Mount Lebanon ... 140
The Mutasarrifate Provincial System (1861-1918) ... 141

Chapter 14. The Realities of War, Famine, and Emigration ... 145
The First World War ... 145
The Locust Plague of 1915 ... 146
The Great Famine of Mount Lebanon ... 147
An Intense Period of Suffering and
Death Leads to Emigration ... 149

Chapter 15. Reaffirming the Homeland—
At the Versailles Conference ... 151
Grand Liban ... 152
The Republic of Lebanon ... 153
The Dual Impact of Emigration ... 154
Ramifications in the New Homelands and Lebanon ... 155
The Long Road Ahead ... 156
Focusing on What Matters ... 157
Success of the Lebanese in their New Homelands ... 158

Chapter 16. Post-Independence Hope and Despair ... 161
The Palestinians in Lebanon ... 162
The Lebanese Civil War ... 164
The Syrian Occupation ... 165
The Rise of Hezbollah ... 166
Continued Instability and the Unending Waves
of Emigration ... 168

Afterword: A Roadmap for Sustained Growth
and Development for Lebanon ... 175

The Shared Future of Lebanon:
A Nation of Pluralism and Unity ... 177
The Need for Secularism in Lebanon's Governance ... 178
A Technocratic Model for Lebanon ... 181
Challenges of Transitioning to a Secular System ... 201
The Future that Awaits ... 202

Works Cited and Consulted
Part One ... 205
Part Two ... 209
Part Three ... 213

Images Credit ... 217
About the Author ... 221

NOTE TO READERS

This book is intended for general readers wishing to know more about Christianity in the country of my birth and reflects my interpretation based on available primary and secondary sources. The content does not intend to endorse or critique any specific religious beliefs. Any references to religious practices, figures, or doctrines are made within historical and cultural contexts. The book is written with respect for all belief systems and should be approached as a scholarly examination of the stated subject matter.

DEDICATION

To those who endured occupation, exile, and hardship with unshakable faith.

You carried the belief across borders and generations.

INTRODUCTION

THIS BOOK IS UNLIKE ANYTHING I have written before. It is not an academic departure, but a deeply personal undertaking. I write as a scholar, albeit in a different field, but also as someone who carries the legacy of a homeland shaped not only by belief, but by centuries of conquest, famine, war, and occupation—events that have left their mark on Lebanese, and many others in the region, across generations. Much of that suffering has been endured by Christians, whose steadfast commitment to their faith made them targets of persecution and displacement. The history I recount here is not abstract. It lives in the memory and experience of many people like me, and in the silent resilience of those who came before us, those who freely accepted a faith, suffered for it, and yet still clung to it.

I approach this task not as a professional historian, but as a witness and descendant. As a scientist, researcher, and academician, I have dedicated my life to the pursuit of knowledge through experimentation, observation, analysis, and evidence. My academic work has been rooted in objectivity, precision, and the discipline of scientific inquiry. It might seem unusual, then, that I now present a book not about science or technology, but about history and religion—subjects that are as complex as they are profound. Yet,

The Enduring Presence of Christianity in Lebanon

there are truths that science alone cannot explain: truths woven into the soul of a people, carried through centuries by conviction, perseverance, and the unspoken strength of identity. This work, for me, represents more than a shift in subject matter. It is a return to something fundamental—something that cannot be measured in laboratories or published in peer-reviewed journals. It is the story of my homeland and the enduring history of my people.

My homeland, Lebanon, lies within the center of what has been called the Levant, a region rich in cultural, religious, and historical significance. It was among the earliest lands in which Christianity was first accepted—where the story of the Gospel took root, where churches were founded in the earliest centuries of the faith, and where the teachings of Christ shaped generations—the Holy Land. This land, revered across religious traditions, holds sacred meaning not only through scripture, but through the lived experiences of the people who have suffered unimaginable trials. For centuries, it has been a birthplace, battleground, and necropolis—all at once—of ideologies, empires, and ambitions. But amid that turbulence, Christianity endured—not as a matter of convenience or cultural habit, but as a source of hope, identity, and survival. Churches were destroyed, languages suppressed, and believers silenced—yet the faith endured. In Lebanon, Christianity has never been merely a tradition; it has often been an act of resistance. Today, churches still stand, prayers are still recited, and hymns still sung— all testimonials to a people who refused to let their faith be extinguished. Even when families were scattered across continents and oceans, communities destroyed, and histories threatened with erasure, their identity persisted.

In a world that often forgets the past in the rush to reinvent the future, I have written this book to ensure that the next generations will remember those who came before them—not just the suffering that they withstood, but their heritage and unwavering spirit. This is not simply a chronicle of a people; it is a testimony. A record of those who lost everything but kept their soul. I hope this book honors them and speaks across time to those who need to remember who they are. It is also a personal offering to my community, to the Christian diaspora from Lebanon and the Levant, and to anyone who values the preservation of faith, culture, and truth—regardless of whose truth it is. In telling this story—often overlooked—I aim to ensure that memory outlives exile. My hope is that readers will gain a deeper understanding of this particular history as a means to understanding the present and perhaps impacting the future.

As the Afterword to this book reveals, I have remained grounded in my scientific training and guided by a commitment to evidence, thoughtful inquiry, and critical analysis of historical sources. I have done my best to uncover facts, understand events in their historical context, and reconcile the conflicting narratives that have emerged, and continue to evolve, over time. I recognize fully that others may arrive at different interpretations, and I respect the possibility—even the inevitability—of disagreement. History, particularly when it spans millennia and touches on deeply held beliefs, rarely speaks in one voice. I am mindful of the fact that many of the themes in this book remain emotionally charged and continue to influence lives today. My intention is not to impose a single narrative, but to offer one rooted in research, sincerity, and lived experiences, with respect for the diversity of perspectives this history naturally evokes.

This is our story. It is sacred, it is fragile, and I am humbled to recount it.

ABOUT THE BOOK

THIS BOOK IS PRIMARILY FOCUSED on the enduring presence of Christianity in Lebanon. It approaches the topic from a strictly historical point of view. However, to understand and appreciate some of the historical events, issues of a theological nature must also be discussed, at least at some depth. As a result, naturally, some readers may disagree with certain content or interpretations. The aim is not to debate these topics, which are best left to trained theologians, but to simply introduce them, as a necessity to cover relevant events.

The history of Christianity in Lebanon begins with Jesus' ministry and continues through the present. Accordingly, it discusses the various entities that had conquered Lebanon's predecessor, Canaan, or Phoenicia, during those times, specifically the Roman and Byzantine empires. The book explains the subsequent spread of Christianity in Lebanon, as well as the congruence of Canaanite thought and Christian theology, which may have contributed to its initial acceptance. Of interest to this history is the subsequent emergence of Maronite Christians in Antioch, their agonizing early period there, the circumstances of their migration to Mount Lebanon, and their eventual adoption of Lebanon as their homeland. Discussed next is the impact of Arab conquests on Christians in Lebanon, starting with the spread of Islam from the Arabian Peninsula into the surrounding lands and the subsequent Muslim Caliphates and dynasties that ruled Lebanon. This is followed by a discussion of Christian schisms, their ramifications for Christianity, and the emergence of the different religious denominations, or sects, now present in Lebanon. Next, we consider the Crusades for the Holy Land and their consequences in Lebanon during and after this period. Then, the return of Muslim rule, after the Crusaders' defeat, under the Mamluk dynasty and Ottoman Caliphate, culminating with the First World War, is discussed. This is followed by a discussion of the central role played by Christians, especially the Maronites, in the formation of modern Lebanon. Then comes an explanation of major Christian migration waves that began during the Ottoman reign and continued through modern times, as well as the successes realized by Lebanese immigrants and their descendants. Finally, the book concludes with an Afterword that reflects on the patterns and consequences of past decisions that may inform the future and offer insights for Lebanon that avoid the repetition of historical mistakes.

Drawing on my scientific training and practice, I have made every effort to ensure a balanced and well-rounded approach, consulting a wide range of scholarly books, peer-reviewed scholarly articles, and respected works from diverse schools of thought. The book also includes a number of biblical quotations that come from the *New Revised Standard Version Bible: Catholic Edition*. Given the nature of the subject, I recognize that numerous interpretations exist, and I have strived to represent these various perspectives accurately, based on a careful integrative approach. My goal has been to offer a comprehensive account and fair analysis based on rigorous investigation, while acknowledging the complexities and nuances inherent in historical inquiry. The arguments I present here are grounded in solid research and sound reasoning, and my conclusions are drawn from the evidence at hand—informed by careful scholarly scrutiny and examination—but I welcome alternative viewpoints and recognize that history is often open to reinterpretation of events. I realize that this subject is one that generates a range of passionate views, and I appreciate the value of the multiple interpretations I have encountered in my research in enriching my understanding of this history. This book represents my views and interpretation, informed by the best available evidence and current scholarly discourse. While other perspectives offer valuable insights, I am satisfied that my reasoning is grounded in the facts and context of the past and present. Of course, I welcome future discussions and research that may illuminate new aspects or provide alternative viewpoints. In the end, I firmly believe in the right of all readers to form their own conclusions.

Some Relevant Calendar Terminologies

This history includes many references to places, people, and dates. Contextual explanations are given regarding people and places when they come up in the discussion. It is important though to say a word about dates and relevant calendars at this point.

There are a number of calendars now in use by different societies, cultures, and religions based on solar and lunar systems for identifying time periods. Of course, there are also some that are no longer in use. Solar calendars are based on the Earth's orbit around the Sun and lunar calendars are based on the Moon's cycles. And there are calendars that combine both solar and lunar aspects. The Hebrew calendar is one example of the lunisolar calendar, where the months are lunar and the years are solar. The Gregorian calendar, solar-based and adopted in AD 1582, is the most widely used calendar today. It replaced the Julian calendar, introduced in 45 BC, although it remains helpful for calculating the dates of floating holidays. Given the subject of this book, the Gregorian calendar, created to establish a Christian chronology, is used. The following terminologies appear often in the book:

BC, *"Before Christ,"* a way of counting years before the birth of Jesus Christ. This calendar system ended at 1.

AD, *"Anno Domini,"* which is Latin for *"In the Year of the Lord,"* refers to the years from the birth of Christ to the present. This calendar system began at 1. The full phrase is *"Anno Domini nostri Jesu Christi,"* which in English means *"In the Year of our Lord Jesus Christ."*

Although the terms BCE (*"Before Common Era"*) and CE (*"Common Era"*) are widely used in academic and secular contexts as religiously neutral alternatives, this book adopts the traditional Christian calendar system: BC *"Before Christ"* and AD *"Anno Domini."* This choice reflects the subject matter of the book, which is rooted in the history of Christianity in Lebanon. To preserve clarity and avoid redundancy, BC and AD will be used primarily in Part One and will be omitted in subsequent sections.

A related periodization issue is the exact date of Jesus Christ's birth, which is not known. Some scholars believe it was between 6 BC and 4 BC; others suggest different dates and ranges. While there is not a *"Year 0"* between the two calendars, for the purpose of our discussion, we assume that Jesus was born in *"Year 0,"* and thus He was crucified in AD 33, approximately.

Because of the Christian-centric focus of the book, the Gregorian calendar is also used in all its sections, including in the section covering the rise of Islam, in Part Two. However, it is similarly important and relevant to say a word about the Hijri Calendar. This is the lunar Islamic calendar: AH, *"Anno Hegirae,"* which is Latin for *"in the year of the Hijrah."* The calendar is used to indicate time within the Islamic era and begins in AD 622, the year the Prophet Muhammad migrated from Mecca to Medina.

PART ONE

From the Canaanites to the Maronites

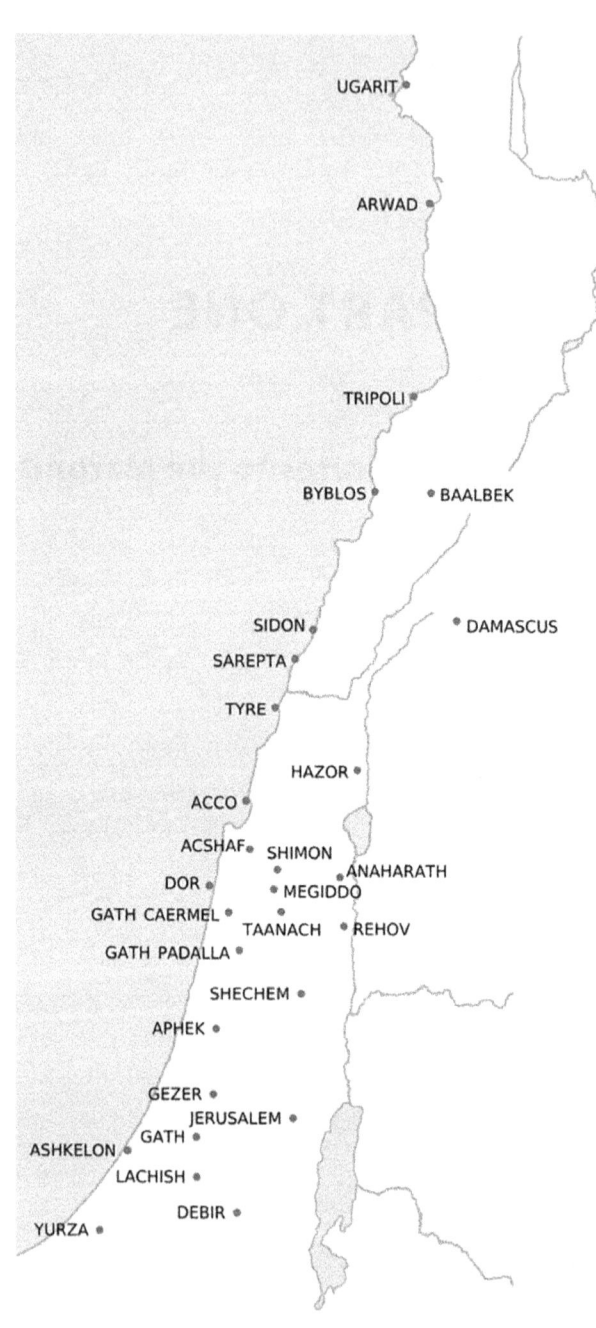

The Land of Canaan

CHAPTER 1.

The Rich Heritage of Ancient Lebanon

LEBANON HAS A LONG HISTORY dating back to biblical times. Its predecessor, Canaan, or Phoenicia, goes even further back into the ancient past. Some of the earliest documented references to the Land of Canaan are inscriptions on the 5,000-year-old clay tablets from Mesopotamia. Emerging around 3000 BC, Phoenicia encompassed much of what is now referred to as the Levant. It was not a unified nation-state by modern definitions, but rather a decentralized network of city-states bound by trade, language, and culture. It reached the height of its influence between 1500 BC and 539 BC, when it fell under Persian occupation. The Phoenician civilization eventually gave way to Hellenistic influence with the arrival of Alexander the Great in 332 BC and then Roman annexation in 64 BC.

The Levant refers to a specific geographic region along the Eastern Mediterranean coast. Starting in the 16th century, European cartographers used the term to describe the Ottoman-controlled territories in this area. The Levant generally includes the modern-day countries of Lebanon, Syria, Jordan, Israel, Palestine, Cyprus, as well as parts of Türkiye (i.e., the Hatay Province), Iraq, and Egypt. Because of its rich connotation of community and related geographical unity, I have used this term for the region throughout the book.

Even before the term "Levant" came into existence, the region was becoming an important trade and commerce focal point for Europe due to its location along the Silk Road. This vital route connected Europe and Asia, facilitating the exchange of spices, textiles, silk, precious metals, and other valuable goods. European commercial interest in the region led merchants to set up trading posts in the Levant as early as the 15th and 16th centuries, essentially becoming the precursors to colonization and foreign control during the 18th and 19th centuries.

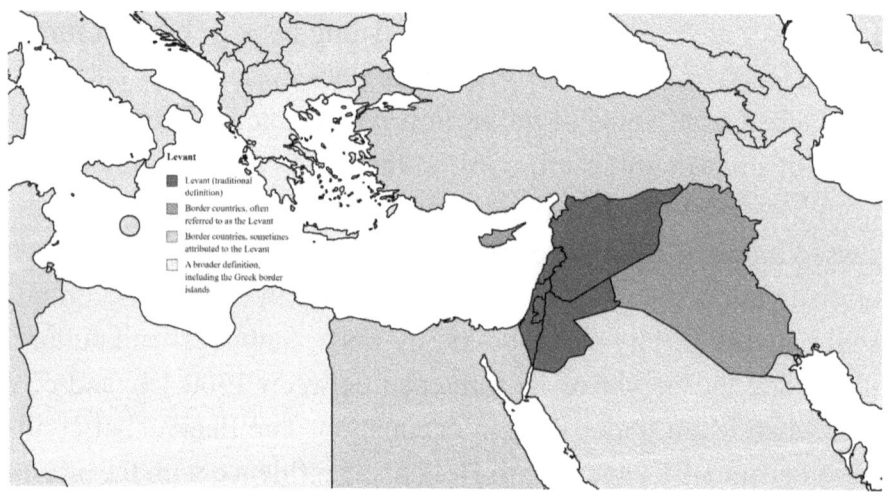

The Levant

Gradually, the terminology used by Europeans to describe the region evolved, particularly during the colonial and imperial eras, when geographic labels were defined relative to Europe. Thus, the lands just east of Europe came to be known as the Near East, where Lebanon fell, while the lands farthest east became the Far East. The Near East encompassed regions geographically broader than the Levant, extending into parts of Türkiye, Iran, the Arabian Peninsula, and North Africa. A new term emerged again in the late

19th and early 20th centuries, Middle East, that now refers to this geographic area as well as additional territories further east.

Lebanon Through the Ages

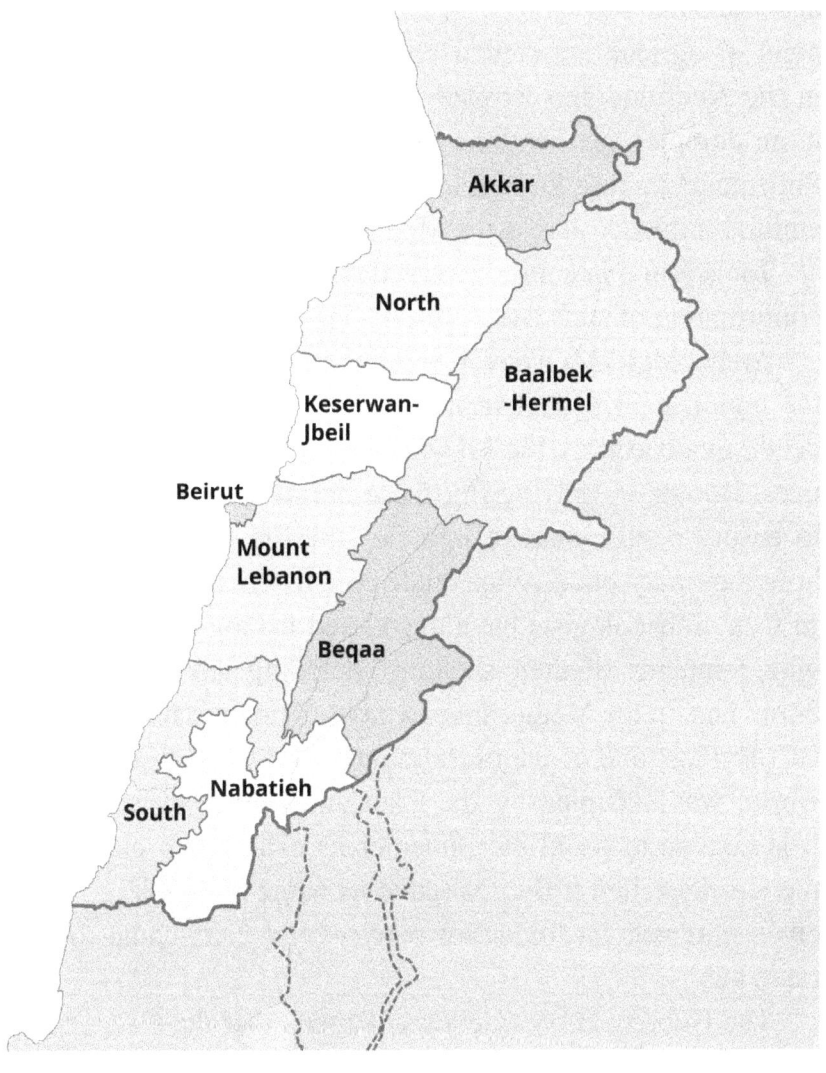

Lebanon

Modern Lebanon is a Mediterranean country situated between Israel to its south and Syria to its north and east. Due to its history and geography, Lebanon is a culturally and religiously diverse nation, with evidence that it was inhabited all through the Stone Age eras of human development from 2.5 million BC to 3000 BC. During this period, societies evolved from using simple stone tools and nomadic subsistence in the Paleolithic era to the establishment of agriculture, settled communities, and early urbanization in the Neolithic and Bronze Ages. This laid the foundations for more complex civilizations, eventually leading to the rise of the Phoenician culture known for its maritime trade, exploration, and cultural influence across the Mediterranean.

Tools found in coastal caves, dating back 50,000 years, provide confirmation of such early presence of humanity in Lebanon.

Archeological discoveries also reveal that communities in the region held beliefs in the afterlife and a soul's journey after death, evidenced by the Phoenicians' religious and funerary practices. Rooted in polytheism, these burial practices were designed to ensure a safe passage into the afterlife and offer insight into how they may have conceptualized existence beyond mortal life. In fact, archaeologists have uncovered fishing communities along with remnants of their shelters, including ancient weapons and burial jars, in the Mediterranean city of Byblos dating back to 9000 BC. Byblos, one of the oldest continuously inhabited cities in the world, was occupied by the Canaanites since at least 4000 BC. It is notable to recall the Phoenicians called their city Gebal, but the Greeks called it Byblos (gave its name to "book") because the city's port was an important papyrus (gave its name to "paper") trade hub.

The Hebrew Bible (Genesis 10) tells that the Canaanites are a group of Semitic-speaking people traditionally regarded as descendants of Canaan, the son of Ham—one of Noah's three sons. Their language is part of the Northwest Semitic branch of the Semitic language family, which also includes Hebrew, Aramaic, and Phoenician. The Canaanites lived on the plains of the Levant, from

Mount Carmel to the Orontes River, a geographic area that today covers all of Lebanon and the northern parts of Israel and Syria. The Canaanites built several coastal cities, in addition to Byblos, that remain in existence today, including Tyre, Sidon, Berytus, Botrys, and Tripoli as well as one inland city, Baalbek. According to Biblical accounts (Judges 3:3), they also inhabited the mountains of Lebanon, the full range, from Mount Hermon to Lebo-Hamath. The Greeks referred to the Canaanites as Phoenicians, which is derived from the Greek word *phoinix*, or "purple-red," for the purple stain they extracted from murex shells to dye the clothes they sold to the ancient world around them. It is also likely a reference to the mythical phoenix, a bird with red, golden, and purple feathers. Dominating the Mediterranean Sea for centuries, the Phoenicians sailed out of their city harbors to trade textiles, olive oil, and wine. But most importantly, the Phoenicians traded timber, from Lebanon's cedar forests, for metals and ivory from Egypt.

More than any other commodity, the cedar trees from the land of Canaan were highly sought after by Phoenician neighbors. In fact, timber from Lebanon's cedar trees was used in building Solomon's temple in Jerusalem around 950 BC. The temple design was influenced by the architectural styles of Phoenician temples, particularly those in the cities of Tyre and Byblos. The Hebrew Bible (1 Kings 7:13-14) also talks about Phoenician influence on the first temple, beyond cedar wood, to include the use of massive stone foundations and fine craftsmanship (1 Kings 5:18), all of which were owed to Solomon's alliance with King Hiram of Tyre.

Solomon turned to the Phoenicians not only because they possessed the best building materials and superior craftsmanship but also because of their advanced architectural knowledge. In addition to their expertise in shipbuilding, the Phoenicians were renowned for their sophisticated building techniques as evidenced by their monumental temples and fortifications. Some scholars also point to shared religious and cultural elements between the ancient

Hebrews and Phoenicians during this period, including the worship of Canaanite deities such as Baal and Asherah.

By about 1200 BC, the Phoenicians were already using their maritime skills to peddle their goods across the whole Mediterranean. To expand their trading business, the Phoenicians sought to colonize commercial outposts all over the Mediterranean. Lacking the interest and military power to sustain and defend large land settlements, they peacefully acquired smaller staging points in support of their trade route. By 1000 BC, they had already established colonies in Spain and North Africa. The Phoenicians also had set up colonies in every major island of the Mediterranean including Cyprus, Sicily, Malta, Sardinia, and Corsica. In 814 BC, the Phoenicians established their most famous colony, Carthage, on the North African coast.

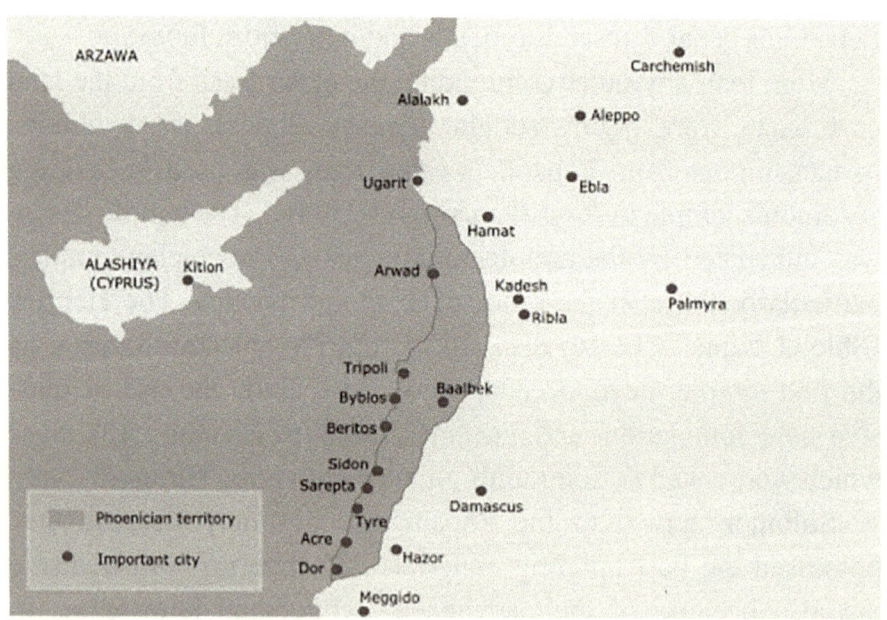

Phoenicia

The Cultures and Religions of Lebanon in the Ancient World

Phoenicia, and Lebanon as its successor, has lived under the rule of many different civilizations. The Phoenicians' preoccupation with trade and their success in opening up markets and outposts for their goods beyond their nation's boundaries left their own borders vulnerable to challenges from other civilizations and dynasties around them. Unlike other ancient civilizations that pursued territorial conquest through warfare, Phoenician expansion was primarily commercial in nature. Their influence spread through the establishment of trading colonies, reflecting a model of peaceful expansion rooted in economic relationships rather than military domination.

Unlike the Phoenicians' own passive colonization, since ancient times, coastal Phoenicia initially, and subsequently Lebanon, has come under the rule of many different conquering cultures that have come and gone, including Assyrians, Babylonians, Persians, Greeks, Romans, Byzantines, Arabs, Crusaders, Mamluks, Ottomans, and French. More recently, others also sought to control this strategic land and its people or seize its resources. Even at the present time, Lebanon remains a target for countries, near and far, though, in every instance, the Lebanese resist, as they have always done, and eventually stave off or repel their conquerors. However, Mount Lebanon, the nucleus hilly territory that was expanded into Lebanon's current boundaries, has traditionally been viewed as a refuge for people escaping persecution in other lands and, for the most part, enjoyed relative isolation and some form of autonomy throughout the periods of foreign rule. This is because of the rugged terrain of the Lebanese mountains, the harsh winter weather, and, most notably, the valiant nature of the inhabitants.

In 875 BC, the Assyrians (875-608 BC) invaded Phoenicia and destroyed the coastal cities of Byblos, Tyre, and Sidon. As the Babylonians (585-539 BC) defeated the Assyrians, much of

Phoenicia fell into their hands. The Persians (539-333 BC) were next to occupy the region, including Phoenicia. The Greeks (333-64 BC) defeated the Persians when Alexander the Great conquered Asia Minor and advanced toward the Phoenician plains. Phoenician cities, except for Tyre, quickly fell under Alexander's rule. The Phoenicians, already engaged in trade with the Greeks, adapted to their rule with ease and were able to continue with their trading uninterrupted.

Soon, a new, but related, power rose after the death of Alexander, when his Empire was divided into Eastern and Southern parts. The Eastern part, including Phoenicia, Asia Minor, Northern Syria, and Mesopotamia, fell to the Seleucid Dynasty, a Macedonian Greek royal family. The Southern part, including Syria and Egypt, fell under the control of the Ptolemaic Dynasty, another Macedonian Greek royal family. Although the Phoenicians were able to hold on to their language during these successive occupations, Greek became the language of literature and cultural expression. This shift accelerated as the coastal regions of the Levant underwent Hellenization following the conquests of Alexander the Great in the late fourth century BC. The main coastal Phoenician cities—such as Tyre, Sidon and Byblos—became centers of Hellenistic culture in the Levant. This cultural landscape continued throughout the Hellenistic period but began to shift following Pompey's capture of Jerusalem in 63 BC, marking the rise of Roman influence in the Eastern Mediterranean.

Prior to its colonization by these various empires, in addition to the Canaanites, the Levant was home to a number of different Semitic people including Jews, Arabs, Philistines, and Arameans, each with its own distinct culture. Under the Roman general Pompey, the land of Canaan was eventually incorporated into the territory of the Roman Empire (64 BC-AD 395) and its successor, the Byzantine Empire (AD 395-636). Residents were granted Roman citizenship. As was the case under Greek rule, the trade activities of the Phoenician cities prospered during the Pax Romana, or Roman Peace. The renewed affluence of Phoenicia spurred new civic and religious developments including transportation systems, palaces, and massive temples. The largest of these structures was at Baalbek, situated atop a high point in the Beqaa Valley, a massive congregate of three temples (for Jupiter, Venus, and Bacchus), three courtyards, and an enclosing structure built of the largest stones ever used by humans. Not only was it the largest edifice in Phoenicia, but it was also the most significant Roman temple ever built, showcasing the wealth and strength of the Roman Empire. The same prosperity also gave rise to intellectual institutions such as the first ever School of Law that was founded in Berytus, which had just been granted Roman colonial status.

The Greek language had become the lingua franca, especially in culture and education, on the Eastern side of the Roman Empire, subsequent to the arrival of Alexander the Great. While Greek influence expanded, the Phoenician language continued to be spoken in everyday life. This began to change under Roman rule, during which the use of Phoenician began to disappear and was eventually supplanted by Aramaic. Although Latin was instituted in official Roman administrative and military settings, it was not immediately adopted by the local populations, especially in Phoenician-speaking areas. Even with increased Roman dominance, the Empire generally maintained a policy of tolerance toward local languages, helping to preserve linguistic diversity during the early phases of governance. While Latin served as the dominant language across all aspects of life in the Western provinces of the Roman Empire, Aramaic was the most widespread language in the Eastern provinces, particularly as the language in everyday life. Aramaic had previously replaced Akkadian as the language of administration and daily use under both the Assyrian and Babylonian empires, where it later became the official language of the Achaemenid Persian Empire.

All three of these civilizations—Assyrian, Babylonian, and Persian—had ruled Phoenicia prior to the Greeks and Romans, contributing to Aramaic's expansion across the region. As Roman dominance began to consume the region, Aramaic functioned as a common language between various ethnic groups in the Levant, especially in trade and communication. As a result, polyglotism became a feature of daily life in the region. In Phoenicia, the native language was retained primarily in religious and cultural contexts, while Aramaic was used for trade and daily communication. Although it was rarely needed by common people, Latin was also used in administration and law. Greek, which had already become deeply integrated into Phoenician cities through centuries of cultural exchange, remained important in their trade and commercial relationships with the Greek city-states. However, by the second century AD, Phoenician was no longer a widely spoken language. Aramaic had fully replaced it and was widely used across the Levant until the rise of Arabic in the seventh century.

Religion played a central role in Phoenician society, shaping its social, political, and economic systems. The Phoenician religion was polytheistic, inspired by the powers of the natural world, with deities assigned to distinct domains that represented nearly every aspect of life and the cosmos—such as wisdom, fertility, and war. As a result, the Phoenicians worshiped a diverse pantheon of gods and goddesses.

Among these deities, El held a prominent place as a revered deity in the broader ancient Semitic pantheon. In the Phoenician tradition, El was often viewed as the supreme deity—the creator and the father of the gods. Next is Baal, born to El—the most important god in the Phoenician culture. Associated with fertility, weather, and agricultural prosperity, Baal played a vital role in religious practice. Anath, sometimes portrayed as Baal's consort, was an influential goddess, known for her protective nature and marital strength. Asherah, El's consort and the mother of Baal, was venerated as a mother goddess and a symbol of fertility. The Hebrew Bible often casts Asherah as a controversial figure (Exodus 34:13-34) and is often depicted as a rival deity to the worship of Yahweh, the God of Israel. There is also Astarte, a goddess of fertility, love, and sexuality, who was seen as a mother goddess associated with nature and reproduction. And Adonis, Astarte's lover, or consort, was god of beauty, fertility, and vegetation, central to Phoenician themes of life, death, and rebirth.

Phoenician religious life centered around temple worship, ritual sacrifices, divination practices, and the worship of deified kings. The Phoenicians often incorporated aspects of other religious beliefs into their own practices. In that they strongly believed in polytheism, the belief systems and deities of the successive civilizations arriving to their shores were similar to what was already in Phoenicia, although known by their local names. This explains why very little changed for them in terms of theology and worship with the arrival of Assyrians, Babylonians, Persians, Greeks, and Romans.

A significant cultural and religious shift soon began to take shape in the first century AD, as a nascent religion, Christianity, was taking hold in the Roman province of Judea—geographically close to the Phoenician coast. Christianity reached Phoenicia early, where, according to the Gospel accounts, Jesus himself visited Phoenician cities and interacted with their citizens. His disciples and apostles continued to visit even after the Crucifixion of Jesus, which took place sometime around 33 AD. Christianity became accepted as a formal religion in Phoenicia during this period even though it was still not sanctioned by the Empire—in fact, it was considered an illegal religion under imperial law. This profound change impacted the resulting culture and religion in the Levant—particularly in Phoenicia and, by extension, in its historical successor, Lebanon. Elements of Phoenician religious thought, especially themes such as life, death, rebirth, and sacrifice, appear to have influenced early Christian theology and symbolism. Christianity, accepted very early in the Land of Canaan, thrived until the seventh century AD, when a new culture and religion emerged.

Strategically located at the crossroads for trade and culture in the Levant, ancient Lebanon was shaped by a succession of civilizations—from the Assyrians to the Romans—each leaving lasting cultural and religious marks over more than a millennium. The Assyrians' imposition of Aramaic set the stage for greater cultural exchange. The Babylonian exile of the Jewish population spurred religious reflection, in contrast to the Persians' more tolerant policies, enabling the return of exiled communities and the reconstruction of the Second Temple.

The Hellenistic culture, spread under Alexander the Great and his successors, brought Greek philosophy and art to Lebanon, as well as collaboration in science and mathematics with the Phoenicians. As Phoenicia also had its own advanced civilization, the intellectual exchange was reciprocal. Roman rule further transformed the region through legal institutions and urban development, leaving a permanent imprint on the architectural and civic landscape of Lebanon.

Lebanon's geography, linking Asia, Africa, and Europe, led to it not only becoming a center of trade but also a dynamic meeting point of different religious traditions. It became a space where established Judaism, emerging Christianity, and, subsequently, rapidly spreading Islam intersected—sometimes in tension, other times in harmony, yet often in ways that enhanced one another's development. This sense of cultural complementarity leads me to believe that the polyglot and pluralistic society reflected in Lebanon today is a mirror of its rich ancient cultural and religious past.

CHAPTER 2.

Lebanon in Biblical History

THE HEBREW BIBLE, ALSO KNOWN as the Tanakh in Judaism and generally referred to as the Old Testament in Christianity, essentially encompasses the same set of religious scriptures, yet is organized slightly differently in each of these two religious traditions. It was written primarily in Hebrew with significant sections written in Aramaic between approximately 1200 BC and 165 BC. This bilingual nature reflects the cultural, political, and historical realities of the Levant during the period in which the different sections and books of the Hebrew Bible were written.

With Aramaic becoming the dominant language during the Assyrian, Babylonian, and Persian empires, its use increasingly influenced Jewish communities—particularly during periods of exile—leading Aramaic to become the Jewish people's primary language of daily communication and religious expression. With the rise of Christianity within a Jewish culture and character, the books of the Hebrew Bible were adopted as the foundational component of the Christian Bible, forming what became the Old Testament.

Observations from the Old Testament

As part of the Southern Levant and an integral part of the biblical landscape, Lebanon falls within the Holy Land, or the "Land of Milk and Honey," a geographic region of significance in Judaism, Christianity, and Islam. Lebanon is referenced in the Old Testament more than seventy times, usually in the context of God's magnificent creation and its beauty, including the cedar forests, mountains, and abundant flora and fauna. Here are some relevant references.

Cedar Trees and Natural Resources—The famous cedars and stones of Lebanon are frequently mentioned (e.g., 1 Kings 5:6, 1 Kings 5:18, Psalm 92:12) as symbols of strength, durability, and beauty:

1 Kings 5:6 – "Therefore command that cedars from the Lebanon be cut for me..."

1 Kings 5:18 – "So Solomon's builders and Hiram's builders and the Gebalites did the stonecutting and prepared the timber and the stone to build the house."

1 Kings 7:2 – "He built the House of the Forest of the Lebanon..."

Psalm 29:5-6 – "The voice of the Lord breaks the cedars; the Lord breaks in pieces the cedars of Lebanon. He makes Lebanon leap like a calf, and Sirion like a young wild ox."

Psalm 92:12 – "The righteous will flourish like the palm tree, and grow like a cedar in Lebanon."

Isaiah 2:13 – "Against all the cedars of Lebanon; lofty and lifted up..."

Ezekiel 31:3 – "Consider Assyria, a cedar of Lebanon, with fair branches and forest shade, and of great height, its top among the clouds."

Ezra 3:7 – *"They gave money to the masons and carpenters, and food, drink, and oil to the Sidonians and Tyrians to bring cedar logs from Lebanon to the sea..."*

Geography and Land—Lebanon is noted for its mountains and lush landscapes (e.g., Deuteronomy 3:25, Song of Solomon 4:8); and, its natural beauty is often used in poetic and prophetic imagery (e.g., Isaiah 35:2, Ezekiel 31:15):

Deuteronomy 3:25 – *"Let me go over, I pray, and see the good land beyond the Jordan, that goodly hill country, and Lebanon."*

Song of Solomon 4:11 – *"Your lips distill nectar, my bride; honey and milk are under your tongue; the scent of your garments is like the scent of Lebanon."*

Hosea 14:6 – *"His shoots shall spread out; his beauty shall be like the olive tree, and his fragrance like that of Lebanon."*

Isaiah 35:2 – *"It shall blossom abundantly, and rejoice with joy and singing. The glory of Lebanon shall be given to it..."*

Isaiah 10:34 – *"He will hack down the thickets of the forest with an axe, and Lebanon with its majestic trees will fall."*

Jeremiah 22:6 – *"For thus says the Lord concerning the house of the king of Judah: 'You are like Gilead to me, like the summit of Lebanon...'"*

Lebanon is frequently mentioned in the Old Testament, often referring to its natural beauty and abundance—most notably its famous cedar forests. These forests were celebrated for their grandeur, strength, and purity, and came to symbolize majesty and resilience in biblical literature. The cedars were highly prized and used in the construction of important structures in Lebanon and the region, including Solomon's Temple in Jerusalem.

Unfortunately, the current reality of Lebanon—marked by political turmoil, sectarian conflict, and economic instability—presents a stark contrast to the idealized biblical imagery. The cedars, once abundant and widely revered, are now limited in number and space due to deforestation and urbanization, serving as a symbol of the country's current environmental vulnerability and endangered cultural heritage. Perhaps the frequent biblical references to Lebanon's landscape may be viewed not only as a spiritual legacy but also a cultural reminder of the land's historical richness and its ongoing struggle.

On one level, biblical references to Lebanon continue to hold a spiritual resonance for those who see the region as central to the religious and cultural history of the Abrahamic faiths. On another level, they serve as a call to reflection—a reminder of the region's historic and symbolic importance and perhaps an invitation to seek restoration: of the land itself and of the peace that once allowed its natural and cultural wealth to flourish. These ancient references serve as a source of hope in the present, pointing toward the enduring potential for renewal—spiritually, politically, and environmentally.

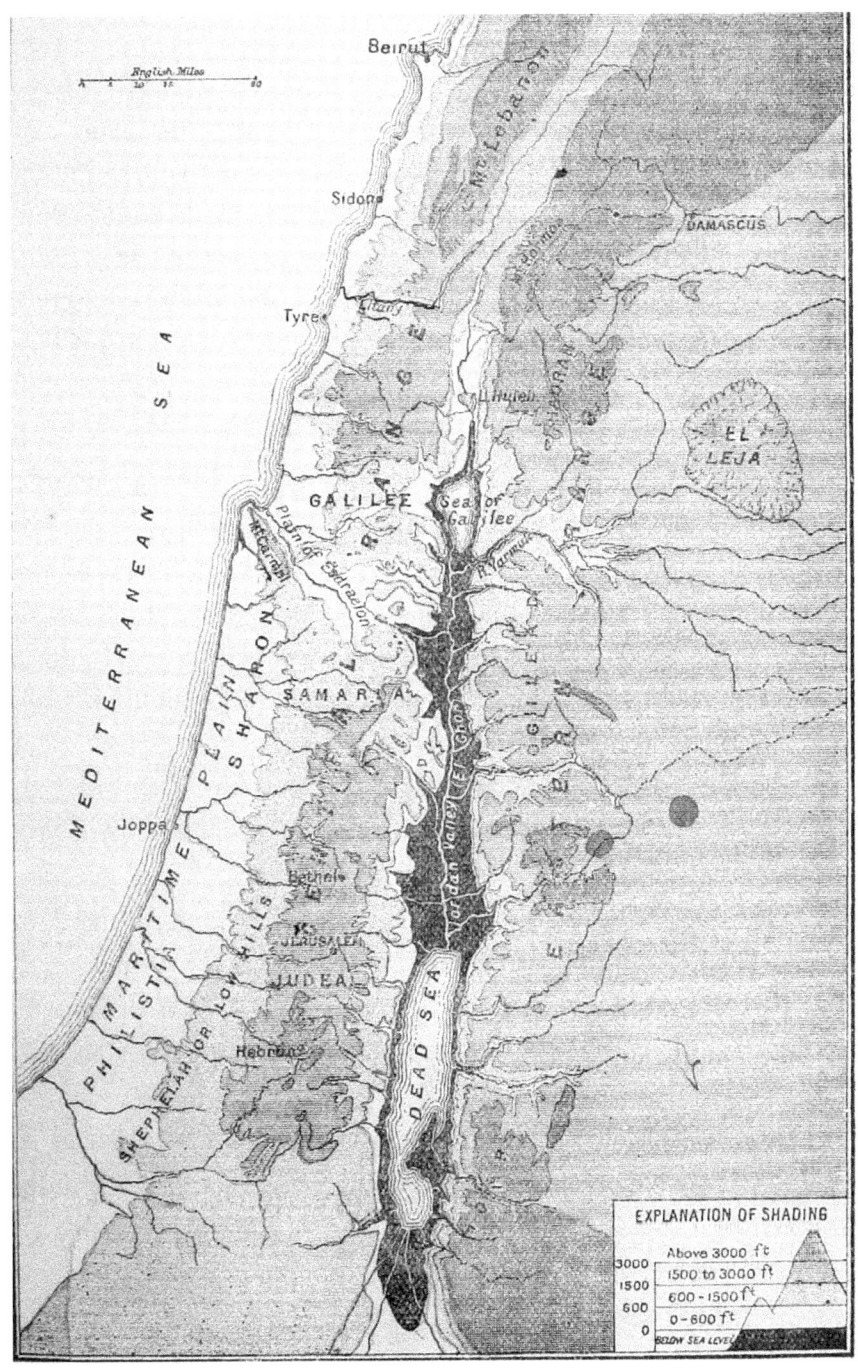

The Holy Land

Observations from the New Testament

The New Testament was written in the first century AD, between the years 50 to 100, in Koine Greek, a language of the Eastern Mediterranean since Alexander the Great (335-323 BC). Although not directly by its name, Lebanon is also often mentioned in the New Testament, particularly with reference to Tyre and Sidon, influential Phoenician cities in the ancient world, as centers of culture and commerce. These cities also played significant roles in the ministry of Jesus. Although the New Testament was written in Greek, Jesus spoke Galilean dialect of Aramaic, the common language in the Phoenician Gentile cities at that time. Jesus often visited there, once encountering a Canaanite woman in Tyre who asked Him to heal her demon-possessed daughter. Jesus obliged, saying to her: *"Woman, great is your faith! Let it be done for you as you wish. And her daughter was healed instantly"* (Matthew 15:28). Then, *"So she went home, found the child lying on the bed, and the demon gone"* (Mark 7:30).

When the Galilean Jewish cities of Chorazin, Bethsaida, and Capernaum rejected Jesus and showed lack of repentance, despite the many miracles He performed among them, Jesus reminded them that He was certain the Gentile cities of Tyre and Sidon would have accepted Him and showed repentance had they witnessed the same miracles. He said: *"But I tell you, on the day of judgment it will be more tolerable for Tyre and Sidon than for you"* (Matthew 11:22).

People from all over the Land of Canaan were drawn to see Jesus in Galilee after hearing about His miracles, including Phoenicians from the cities of Tyre and Sidon. They flocked to Him: *"…hearing all that he was doing, they came to him in great numbers from Judea, Jerusalem, Idumea, beyond the Jordan, and the region around Tyre and Sidon"* (Mark 3:8). And: *"He came down with them and stood on a level place, with a great crowd of his disciples and a great multitude of people from all Judea, Jerusalem, and the coast of Tyre and Sidon*" (Luke 6:17).

Another glorious, and also lighthearted, encounter with Jesus in Lebanon, as relayed in the New Testament, is the "The wedding at Cana." Cana, or Qana, is a small town in the Northern Galilee, within today's South Lebanon, believed to be where Jesus performed his first miracle of turning water into wine. It goes as follows:

Jesus' mother said to him:

"*They have no wine.*"

Jesus replied:

"*…My hour has not yet come.*"

His mother said to the servants:

"*…Do whatever he tells you.*"

Then Jesus said to servants:

"*…Fill the jars with water.*"

They filled them to the brim. Then He told them:

"*…Now draw some out, and take it to the steward of the feast.*"

They did, and the steward of the feast tasted the water-turned-into-wine. He did not realize where it had come from, though the servants knew. Then he called the bridegroom aside and said:

"*…Every man serves the good wine first; and when men have drunk freely, then the poor wine; but you have kept the good wine until now*" (John 2:3-10).

While Jesus' ministry centered in Galilee among Jews, the New Testament references to Gentiles in Tyre, Sidon, and in other

Canaanite cities build on Old Testament themes, emphasizing God's care and Jesus' love for all humanity.

The New Testament references to Lebanon and its cities, particularly Jesus' visits to Tyre and Sidon, carry both historical and theological significance for Lebanon. They are noteworthy because He was stepping into a Gentile territory, a remarkable moment in the expansion of the gospel beyond traditional Jewish communities. For example, the Encounter with the Canaanite woman in Tyre, who pleads for Jesus to heal her demon-possessed daughter, demonstrates that faith transcends ethnic and religious boundaries. The story serves as a model for faith that is not bound by race, nationality, or historical divisions.

This is even more meaningful in a contemporary reflection, especially in the context of Lebanon's modern-day situation. As a culturally and religiously diverse society—one of the most pluralistic in the region—such stories underscore the importance of cross-cultural engagement. Lebanon's long history of both coexistence and conflict makes it a natural and symbolic place for reflecting on these teachings. They offer insights into how faith can bridge divisions and lessons in inclusivity, where sectarian divisions have historically fueled tension.

This encounter in Tyre serves as a call to dismantle social, cultural, and religious barriers, encouraging engagement with people from all walks of life. In Lebanon, both in Tyre and across the country, this message continues to hold significance for promoting peace and reconciliation. Even amidst the country's political instability, economic crisis, and religious tensions, healing is still possible, not only through political reform but also through individual and collective efforts.

Early Christianity and the Spread of the Gospel in Lebanon

Christianity found acceptance in Lebanon from the earliest days of the faith. The rapid spread of Christianity in Phoenicia can be rightfully attributed to disciples such as the Apostle Paul. However, even though Jesus started His ministry in the Galilean city of Capernaum and among Jews, the Phoenicians had routine direct contact with Him, which explains why they were among the first Gentiles to accept Christianity. The fact that Jesus had visited the cities of Tyre and Sidon, where people came out to hear Him preach, as reported by the apostles, is another reason for this acceptance (Matthew 15:21, Mark 3:8, Mark 7:24, Luke 6:17).

Jesus' final words, shortly before He ascended into heaven, known as "The Great Commission," were a most impactful call to action: *"Go therefore and make disciples of all nations, baptizing them in the name of the Father and of the Son and of the Holy Spirit..."* (Matthew 28:19). The Apostle Paul, also called Saint Paul, was one who responded to this call, according to Acts—the fifth book of the New Testament, narrating the founding of the Christian Church and the spread of its message to the Roman Empire. Paul began his formal missionary journey with Barnabas, a Jewish native of Cyprus and an early Christian disciple in Jerusalem, in approximately AD 47, although there is reference to his earlier passing through Phoenicia shortly after his conversion to Christianity around AD 36. His mission travels brought him to nearby Phoenicia but also took him to Greece, Antioch, Asia Minor, and Rome.

Paul was not one of the original twelve disciples of Jesus; he was called to be an apostle after Jesus' ascension into heaven. In fact, before becoming Paul, he was Saul, and a Pharisee who persecuted Christians. While he was on such a mission to Damascus, Paul experienced an encounter with Jesus that changed his life. This led to his baptism and the start of his mission, preaching the gospel to the Gentiles. With the New Testament being written in Greek, and Paul's fluency in the Greek language, literature, and culture, this enabled him to communicate naturally with a large number of Gentiles who spoke the language. Of course, Paul was also fluent in Aramaic, the native language of the time, in addition to being able to read and write in Hebrew. He was actually schooled in Jewish law. Furthermore, as a Roman citizen by birth, and an educated person, it is assumed that Paul spoke Latin, at least to some extent. Even though Latin was the official language of Rome, Paul wrote his letters to citizens of the Roman Empire in Greek because the predominant language in the Eastern side of the Empire was Greek.

As he traveled, not surprisingly, Tyre and Sidon were on his itinerary too. The Apostle Paul visited Tyre during his missionary journeys and lived with welcoming Christians in the city. During one of the visits, fearing for his life, they wanted him to stay and not return to Jerusalem: "*We came in sight of Cyprus; and leaving it on our left, we sailed to Syria and landed at Tyre, because the ship was to unload its cargo there. We looked up the disciples and stayed there for seven days. Through the Spirit they told Paul not to go on to Jerusalem*" (Acts 21:3-5). Paul experienced opposition in Jerusalem because of his work on behalf of Christianity.

Paul's connection to Sidon was equally strong. Around AD 60, Paul was a prisoner on a ship heading to Rome when he was allowed by the centurion to make a stop in Sidon and visit with the Christians on his way: "*The next day we put in at Sidon; and Julius treated Paul kindly, and allowed him to go to his friends to be cared for*" (Acts 27:3).

The Phoenician cities of Tyre and Sidon offer early evidence of fulfilling the Great Commission by spreading the Gospel outside of traditional geographical Jewish communities.

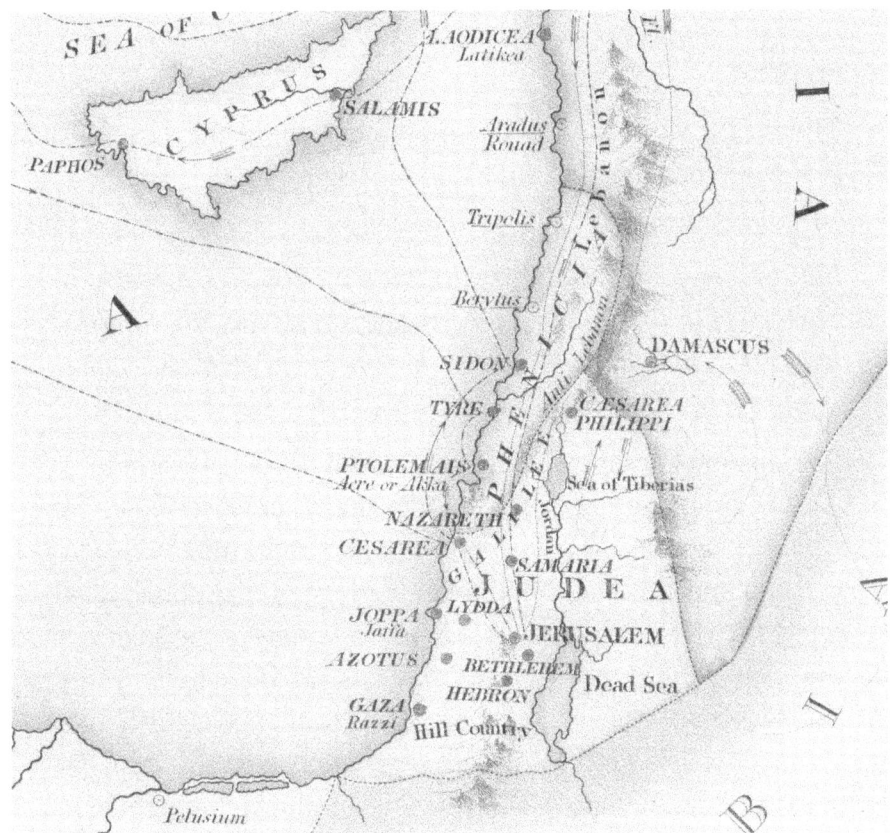

The Great Commission—Travels of St. Paul

Phoenician Thoughts and Christian Theology

Similarities between Phoenician thoughts and Christian theology may explain the popularity of Christianity among early Phoenicians. A God who sacrificed his only begotten son must have sounded very familiar to the Phoenicians. From Cory's *Ancient Fragments*:

> *"For Cronus, whom the Phoenicians call Il, and who after his death was deified and instated in the planet which bears his name, when king, had by a nymph of the country called Anobret an only son, who on that account is styled Ieoud,*

for so the Phoenicians still call an only son: and when great dangers from war beset the land he adorned the altar, and invested this son with the emblems of royalty, and sacrificed him."

There is a similarity in this statement about the Greek Titan Cronus from the New Testament about Jesus Christ:

"For God so loved the world that he gave his only Son, so that everyone who believes in him may not perish but may have eternal life. Indeed, God did not send the Son into the world to condemn the world, but in order that the world might be saved through him" (John 3:16-17).

Perhaps the Phoenicians did not need much persuasion in order to accept Christianity because the two shared at least one common core belief: sacrifice. An example of the similarities between the Phoenician and Christian thought is the legend of Adonis' death—Astarte's lover—whose death and symbolic rebirth are said to have occurred in the hills overlooking Byblos. In Phoenician religion, Adonis was associated with the cycles of death and rebirth, reflecting broader spiritual themes that also appear in different forms within Christian theology. This story is similar to the personal life of sacrifice and subsequent resurrection of Jesus. As the Phoenician legend goes, Adonis was a Phoenician god who died in a boar fight while hunting near a river and is resurrected every year along with the beautiful and colorful spring vegetation of the hills and plains of Byblos. This seasonal cycle was interpreted in both ritual and religious terms—the god's death in winter marked the start of a mourning period, while his rebirth in the spring was celebrated as a symbol of renewal and the return of life.

The cultural merging between the Phoenician religion and Christianity was a gradual process, shaped by geography, history, and the Roman Empire. It began subtly during Jesus' own lifetime, when He and His disciples visited Phoenician cities and engaged with local populations. As Christianity continued to develop in its early centuries and spread throughout the region under Roman rule, it gained acceptance in Phoenicia, harmoniously co-existing with, and in some respects absorbing, elements of the surrounding religious environment. This reached new heights in AD 313, when Christianity moved from a marginalized faith to a legally recognized religion of the Roman Empire under the Edict of Milan.

The myth of Adonis' death and rebirth was commemorated through seasonal festivals in antiquity, in which his death was lamented and his rebirth celebrated. The story of Adonis continues to be celebrated as a reminder of the Phoenicians' rich spiritual heritage embedded in Lebanon's heritage. When the reddish winter melting snow and rain runoff flows downward from the mountains of Afqa above Byblos and into the Adonis Valley, this is said to be the blood of Adonis.

I remember, as a young boy, participating in spring festivals organized by the Adonis Club in Byblos, also known as Jbeil, that reenacted the mythical legend of the Phoenician god Adonis—who, according to tradition, died while battling a wild boar near the River of Ibrahim, once known as the Adonis River. This river flows close to Byblos, the city where I grew up. These simple celebrations gave new life to ancient myths. I vividly recall helping build floats and decorate vehicles that retraced Adonis' path from the river's source in Afqa, high in the Lebanese mountains, and continuing down to its mouth, where it merges with the Mediterranean Sea. Unbeknownst to me then, these processions echoed ancient mourning festivals held by the Phoenicians in honor of the youthful god beloved by the goddess Astarte. The route from Afqa to Byblos, which we retraced on foot, served as a living link between ancient myth and modern memory. These rituals reflected Lebanon's layered identity—Phoenician, Roman, Byzantine, Christian, and Muslim—each contributing to the country's rich and complex cultural and religious tapestry.

CHAPTER 3.

Christianity in Lebanon under the Roman and Byzantine Empires

CREDIT FOR PAVING CHRISTIANITY'S WAY in Lebanon is given to Saint Paul, who spent time during his gospel mission in Phoenicia, starting around AD 47. This advancement of Christianity occurred despite the fact that the Romans, in these early periods, had proclaimed Christianity a threat to the Roman Empire because the Christians refused to worship the emperor, who was considered to be a god. The Romans also questioned the Christians' loyalty to Rome for their refusal to serve in the military or subscribe to any of the prevailing traditions and beliefs they espoused.

While conditions improved significantly for Christians after Christianity became the official religion in the Roman Empire, change was soon on the horizon. After the fall of the Western Roman Empire in AD 476, the Levant—including present-day Lebanon—came under the authority of the Byzantine Empire, moving the center of governing from Rome to Constantinople. Christianity, in its Eastern tradition, became even stronger under Byzantine rule. However, this period was mired by Christological disputes—particularly debates over the nature of Christ—that caused divisions within Eastern Christianity and the Empire.

These theological rifts contributed to the conditions preceding the Islamic conquests in the seventh century, which transformed Lebanon's religious and cultural landscape and began a new era in Levantine history. Most of Lebanon came under complete Muslim rule quickly, with the exception of its mountainous regions, where communities retained a degree of autonomy. This marked another significant religious and cultural transformation, with Arabic gradually replacing Greek and Aramaic as the new dominant language in the Levant.

The Roman Empire

Phoenicia came under Roman rule in 64 BC as part of Pompey's Province of Syria. The Roman Empire (27 BC-AD 476), one of the most influential governing systems in history, controlled the Mediterranean basin, large swaths of Europe, Western Asia, and North Africa. Rome was its capital from inception to demise. Under its rule, ending in AD 395, residents of Phoenicia were granted Roman citizenship.

The first two centuries of the Empire saw a period of unprecedented stability and prosperity attributed to the Pax Romana that, in part, is credited for facilitating the spread of the gospel. In fact, we know that on his return trip to Jerusalem from Rome, Greece, and Asia Minor, Paul made a famous stop in the harbor of Tyre and inaugurated an already formed Church in AD 58 for a small community of Christians living in the Phoenician city. Additional conversions among the Phoenicians followed, giving the Church of Tyre significant presence and warranting the appointment of the city's own Bishop by the end of the second century. Also, similar to Tyre and Sidon, conversions were happening in the other Phoenician cities of Byblos, Berytus, Botrys, and Tripoli.

In AD 286, a soft-split of the Roman Empire by Emperor Diocletian (AD 284-305) created the Eastern and Western empires, each having its own ruler. An Eastern part, Byzantine, ruled by

Diocletian himself with allegiance to Byzantium and a Western part that kept its affiliation with Rome, ruled by Maximian (AD 286-305). At the time, this division did not constitute the formation of two separate sovereign states but rather served to improve administrative efficiency across the empire. In AD 306, the Emperor Constantine the Great (AD 306-337) came into power. He converted to Christianity in AD 312 and issued the Edict of Milan in AD 313, recognizing Christianity throughout the Empire. The numbers of Christians grew significantly soon after Constantine's conversion to Christianity. Finally, the Edict of Thessaloniki, issued in AD 380 by Emperor Theodosius I, banned polytheism and made Christianity the official religion of the Empire. In Phoenicia, however, Christianity co-existed harmoniously with the Phoenician religion, presumably because of some overlapping beliefs, for the first three centuries.

The area that is now Lebanon was part of the Roman Empire for much of the first to fourth centuries AD. In AD 395, after several unifications and divisions, the Roman Empire was firmly split into two independent empires, Byzantine, affiliated with Constantinople, formerly the city of Byzantium, and Roman, which naturally kept its affiliation with its founding city, Rome. Lebanon continued to function seamlessly under the rule of the Byzantine Empire.

Under the Roman Empire in the Levant, Jewish communities initially enjoyed relative autonomy and freedom to practice their religion but faced increasing tensions, persecution, and displacement due to revolts and Roman suppression. Early on, under Constantine and his successors, the Empire had laws restricting Jewish religious activities but were allowed to practice their faith under certain legal and social limitations. Despite this tension and repression, the Jews contributed to the Empire's economy, culture, and intellectual life. Jewish communities were active in agriculture, trade, and crafts, and some in taxation policies and systems. Communities in Galilee and Judea were hubs of commerce that sustained the local and regional economies. Jewish learning institutions and scholars created Rabbinical foundations that preserved Jewish identity under Roman rule. These scholarly efforts also contributed to a broader philosophical discourse, some of which intersected with the intellectual and religious bases that Christianity emerged from.

The Byzantine Empire

In AD 330, even before the final split, solidifying the strength of the Eastern half of the Empire, Constantine moved the capital of the Roman Empire to the ancient city of Byzantium and renamed it Constantinople, becoming the first Emperor of the Byzantine Empire. Situated between Europe and Asia, Byzantium was first settled in the seventh century BC by the Greeks.

Although the Roman Emperor Constantine the Great converted to Christianity in AD 312, the people of Phoenicia, living under Roman rule at the time, were already well ahead of him. The Acts of the Apostles speaks of much earlier Christian presence in Phoenicia. During the fourth century, Sidon and Tyre were active on the Christian scene. In AD 325, the Christian Bishop of Sidon attended the Council of Nicaea and in AD 335, a council was held in Tyre, signifying the role of Tyre as one of the most important Christian cities of that era. This may explain why, during earlier periods, Christian bishops of coastal Lebanese regions held the honorary title Metropolitan of Phoenicia Maritima, reflecting the historical significance of Phoenicia in early Christianity.

From AD 395 forward, the Eastern and Western halves of the Empire were being ruled as fully independent states. In AD 476, the Western Roman Empire came to its end. Following the division of the Roman Empire, Lebanon came fully under Byzantine control. During this time, the Christian community faced various theological debates, including those related to Christology, which would later influence different Christian denominations and lead to a number of schisms, and smaller religious sects, initially within the Eastern churches but also subsequently in the Western Church.

By the fifth century AD, Christianity had spread widely in the two empires and was a well-organized religion. It comprised five founding patriarchates, or ecclesiastical sees, in significant cities: Rome, Alexandria, Antioch, all three created in the first century; Constantinople, fourth century, and Jerusalem, fifth century. Rome is the only Patriarchate in the Western Roman Empire. Each Patriarchate was governed under the authority of a bishop, with Rome holding primacy. The Church of Antioch, which began with Saint Peter, was closest, geographically and culturally, to Lebanon and was considered the governing authority for the Christians in Lebanon.

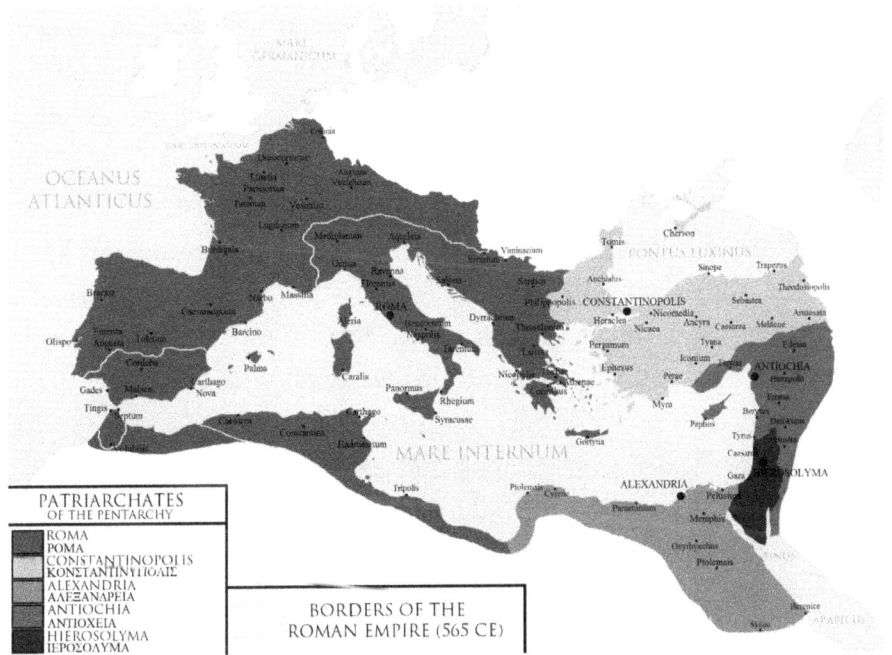

The Five Ecclesiastical Sees
(Rome, Constantinople, Alexandria, Antioch, and Jerusalem)

With this church organization centered around the five different Patriarchates, a dual national and religious identity began to form in the coastal and mountainous parts of Lebanon during this period, with coastal cities accepting the Byzantine culture and holding on to the Greek language, and the mountain communities continuing to embrace the Syriac traditions. Similarly, the Aramaic language was becoming even more common, at the expense of the Phoenician language, indicating the start of a transformation from Phoenicia to Lebanon. Syriac, a dialect of the Aramaic language, emerged in the first century AD, becoming the lingua franca in the region for many centuries to come.

The name Lebanon appears in Mesopotamian and Egyptian records as early as 2500 BC, often in relation to the region's cedar wood trade. Although not yet defined as a political region, the name "Lebanon" began to emerge by the early fifth century AD as a designation for a subset area within the Land of Canaan. It was primarily used to describe the mountain ranges encompassing Mount Lebanon and Anti-Lebanon.

Throughout the Byzantine period, a visible Jewish community lived on the Phoenician coast in cities like Beirut, Sidon, and Tyre. After the spread of Christianity, Jews lived alongside Christians, polytheists, and other groups, each practicing their own faith. However, they still faced periodic persecution, especially in the later stages of the Byzantine Empire, with increased anti-Jewish sentiments—forced conversions and expulsions. Byzantine rulers also enacted laws that limited Jewish religious activities, and there were occasional outbreaks of anti-Jewish violence, which at times intensified, particularly as the empire sought to enforce Christianity.

Antioch

Christianity in Lebanon cannot be fully understood and appreciated without understanding Antioch's significance during the

Roman and Byzantine Empires. Strategically positioned at the crossroads of Asia and the Mediterranean and situated on the banks of the Orontes River, Antioch of Syria, as it was known then, is now called Antakya in the Hatay Province of Southern Türkiye. The dwellers of ancient Antioch identified themselves as Greeks, Romans, Jews, and Syriacs. Thus, its importance was seen in trade, culture, and diversity. However, Antioch's religious impact cannot be underestimated.

In early Christianity, Antioch became central in Paul's ministry and theological development of the Gentiles and is often referred to as the *"Cradle of Christianity,"* as described in Acts 11:26:

"...Then Barnabas went to Tarsus to look for Saul, and when he had found him, he brought him to Antioch. So it was that for an entire year they met with the church and taught a great many people, and it was in Antioch that the disciples were called 'Christians'."

The Patriarchate of Antioch, which first began with Saint Peter, was the governing entity for Christians in Lebanon and remains so for a number of denominations through this time, although none are physically administered out of the current city of Antakya.

Laying the Foundations at Beit Mārūn

In the fourth century AD, with the growth of Christianity continuing in the coastal regions of Phoenicia, a similar expansion was already taking place nearby. A Syriac Christian monk by the name of Maron, or Mārūn in Syriac (AD 350-410), was a man of faith, humility, and devotion to God. Disenchanted with the ongoing divisive theological debates of his time, he shed a life of comfort to live as a hermit, embracing austerity in the open air and dedicating himself to prayer, fasting, and spiritual healing on the mountains of Cyrrhus in Antioch, near the city of Aleppo in today's Syria. He was on the move, along with hundreds of other monks and thousands of their Christian followers, who were seeking asceticism and attracted to his holiness and reported ability to perform miracles. They were also fleeing persecution over a number of Christological differences with other Christian groups, the most serious of which concerned the nature of Christ's divinity and humanity.

According to estimates, Saint Maron died around AD 410. Now a saint, Maron left behind a community of believers focusing on a spiritual life, devoting itself to prayer, fasting, and contemplation away from worldly distractions. This community of Christian faith had a unique identity, defined beliefs, and established practices. Before Saint Maron, these people, who would later become known as Maronites, were part of the greater Christian community in the Antioch region. To honor him, and with help from the Byzantine Emperor Marcian (AD 450-457), his disciples built a monastery in AD 452 named for him. This monastic and spiritual community near Antioch was rooted in his teachings and became known as the Beit Mārūn, or House of Maron, community. The monastery continued to gain imperial recognition from successive emperors, including under Emperor Justinian I (AD 527-565), who supported church constructions and theological education. The Monastery of Beit Mārūn eventually became a hub for theological, spiritual, and cultural activities serving hundreds of monks and thousands of followers.

The Ecumenical Council of Chalcedon

The Council of Chalcedon, held in AD 451 was called by Emperor Marcian to resolve debates about the nature of Christ and reasserting the two distinct natures in one person, Dyophysitism, against doctrines that viewed Christ's divine and human natures as solely divine, Monophysitism, or as an undivided union of divine and human nature, not two distinct, Miaphysitism.

In addition to affirming that Jesus is fully human and fully divine—one person in two natures—the Council also declared that Mary is Theotokos, "God-bearer." It further clarified earlier changes in the Nicene Creed regarding the dual nature of Jesus as well as the addition of *"and the Son,"* referred to as the *"Filioque"* in Latin, as follows: "*... I believe in the Holy Spirit, the Lord, the giver of life, who proceeds from the Father and the Son, who with the Father and the Son is adored and glorified, who has spoken through the prophets...*"

Thus, a first serious split in Christianity resulted from the Council of Chalcedon and, shortly after, giving rise to new autonomous churches in Antioch and Alexandria, along the lines of Chalcedonian and non-Chalcedonian Christology. The Chalcedonians became the Antiochene Greek Orthodox Church of Antioch ("Greek" refers to the exclusive recognition by the Byzantine Empire), now part of the Eastern Orthodox Church, and subsequently the Antiochene Syriac Maronite Church. The non-Chalcedonians became known as the Oriental Orthodox Christians, including the Syriac Orthodox Church, the Armenian Apostolic Church, and the Coptic Orthodox Church of Alexandria.

Those who accepted the Council's decrees were called Melkites, or imperials, as loyalists to the emperor. Disagreements between the Melkites and the Oriental Orthodox Christians set the stage for the eventual separation.

In the end, the diversions resulting from the Council of Chalcedon proved to be pivotal in Christian history, leading to a significant doctrinal split. These long-lasting divisions between those who accepted the Council's decisions and those who rejected them have gone beyond theological and religious disputes to include geographic, linguistic, cultural, political, and social identities that continue to shape Christians in the Eastern and Western churches.

Reflecting on the Byzantine Empire, I find myself intrigued by its pivotal place in Christian history, especially in shaping some of the most fascinating and enduring branches of the faith. No state or city captures this more fully than Byzantium and Antioch—centers of theological thought, spiritual vitality, and ecclesiastical identity during the Church's formative centuries. The Byzantine Empire was the custodian of Christian thought and practice for over a millennium. Antioch was a patriarchal see where Christianity's most fundamental doctrines were shaped. Perhaps this connection is no coincidence, given my heritage as the child of Melkite and Maronite parents.

The Melkites, aligned historically with the Chalcedonian orthodoxy of the Byzantine Empire and Church authority, preserved the Greek-Antiochene theological and liturgical heritage, even as they adapted to other parts of the world. The Maronites, born from a monastic movement in the Antiochene and Lebanese mountains, developed along a more isolated path, retaining their strong Syriac roots. Proud of my Lebanese heritage, shaped by both Greek and Syriac legacies, I am inspired by how both communities have endured and persevered for centuries.

CHAPTER 4.

The Maronites

THE MARONITES ARE CREDITED WITH founding the modern Lebanese entity, shaping its current geography, political system, and borders as they were defined in 1920, during the French Mandate period following the First World War. They have a history of resilience, adaptation, and contributions to Lebanon's cultural, political, and social fabric. Anchored in Lebanon, the Maronites are present all over the world. The head of the Antiochene Syriac Maronite Church, the Patriarch of Antioch and All the East, is elected by the bishops of the Maronite Church and now resides in Bkerké, Lebanon. While Syriac is no longer the exclusive language for the Maronites, it has remained their liturgical language. However, the path to establishing their own homeland has been fraught with distress, danger, and determination. This legacy of faith and survival is responsible for the enduring presence of Christianity in Lebanon.

Keeping and Growing the Faith

By the fifth century, these Syriac-speaking Christians had developed into a strong and visible Maronite community of believers, in many parts of Antioch of Syria and other places where the language was not a barrier, even beyond their Antiochene base. As such, they were also impacting the Byzantine Empire religiously through their missionary work. Just as significant, the good name of Saint Maron before his death and the labor of the Beit Mārūn community after his death had already been yielding fruit in nearby Mount Lebanon, where many inhabitants were converting to Christianity at the hands of Saint Maron disciples. This brought the Syriac communities of Antioch and Mount Lebanon even closer. By then, the Aramaic language and Syriac dialect had spread far, becoming a common language in much of the Byzantine Empire, and overtaking the Phoenician language in the cities and mountains of Lebanon. However, Greek was still the dominant language of the Empire.

The theological differences that came to a head after the 451 Council of Chalcedon, causing a split in the Church of Antioch, did not let up, though. To the contrary, the animosity and resentment continued for many more years to come. As a result, the community of Beit Mārūn was enduring difficult conditions caused by a multitude of circumstances including political oppression by some fellow Byzantines over religious dogma and the intense anti-Chalcedonian sentiments in Antioch. Even though the Maronites' fidelity to Chalcedonian Christology caused tension with Christians of opposing views, their movement was thriving around the Orontes River—a major river in the Levant, with historical, cultural, and geopolitical significance, beginning in Lebanon's Beqaa Valley, flowing unusually northward through Syria, and ending in Türkiye, where it empties into the Mediterranean Sea near Antioch—with their major monastery named after their patron continuing to attract clergy and followers.

By the early sixth century, as their numbers in Antioch and Mount Lebanon grew, the Maronites had evolved into a religious group with an organization and hierarchy that included bishops. They also built additional monasteries throughout the region. However, in 517, an astonishingly violent attack on the Maronites in Apamea, a town near Antioch in today's Syria, also on the banks of the Orontes River, caused the martyrdom of 350 Maronite monks, slayed for their Chalcedonian beliefs by other Christians. This incident, literally, put the fear of God into the hearts of the Maronite community.

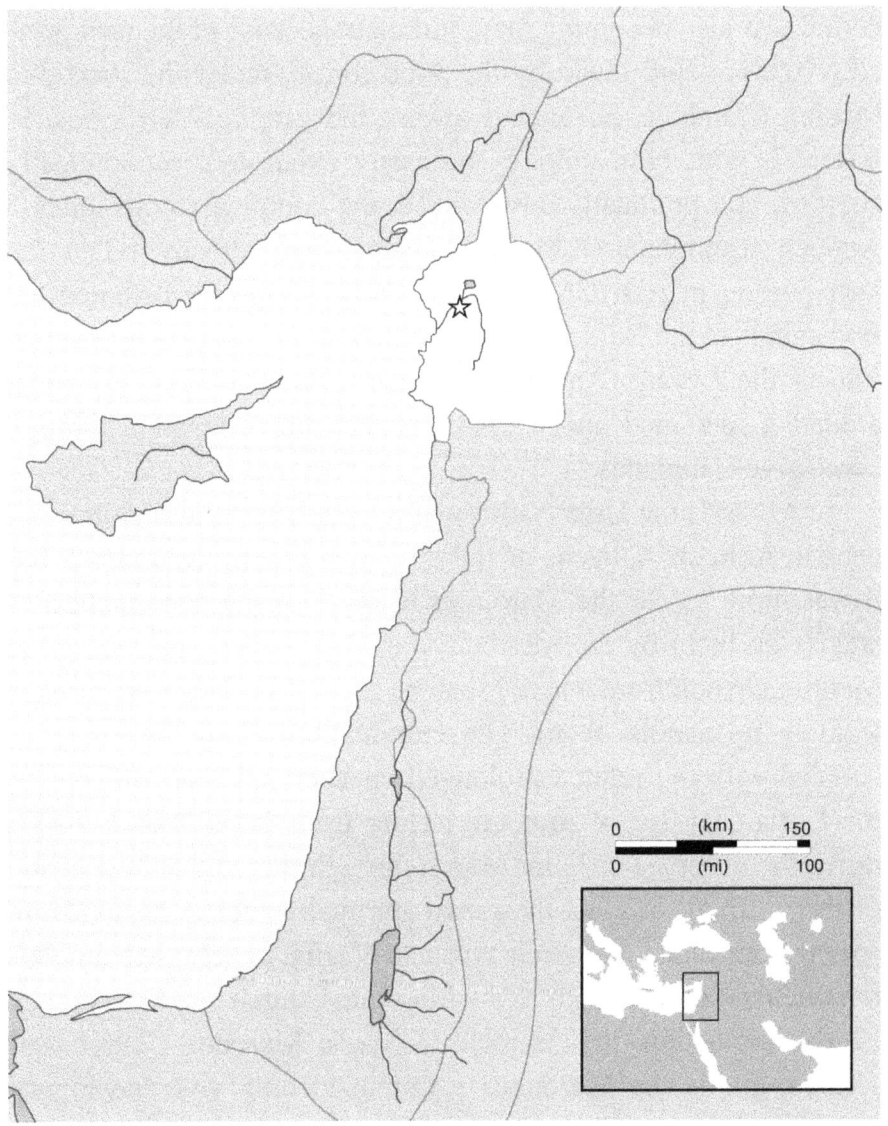

Antioch

A Bold Move—First Patriarch for the Maronites

During the seventh century AD, the Antioch region in particular, and the Byzantine Empire in general, were going through a difficult period, primarily because of a lingering war between the Byzantines and Sassanian-Persians (AD 602-628). However, this period was also becoming more turbulent because of the unexpected progress being made by the Arab forces, under the Rashidun Muslim Caliphate, advancing toward the Empire's territories. In AD 637, with both empires militarily exhausted, economically strained, and politically destabilized, the conquest troops entered Antioch triumphantly. Mount Lebanon had already fallen the year before, in AD 636, after the Arabs decisively defeated the Byzantines at the Battle of Yarmouk, effectively ending Byzantine rule in the Levant. Antioch and much of the Byzantine region around it remained under Arab and Muslim occupation through successive Caliphates.

In AD 661, the Umayyad Muslim Caliphate solidified its presence in Antioch. Citizens of the city were uneasy as a result, but it was more so for the Maronites because of the continuation of attacks on them by the Monophysites over beliefs, as well as on Mount Lebanon from where Muslims and Byzantines were already teaming up against them. The culmination of all these events, coupled with the related prolonged vacancy, or *Sede vacante*, in the Patriarchal See of Antioch, lasting from AD 684 to AD 687, drove the disciples of Saint Maron through the unilateral decision of their bishops to elect their own spiritual leader. A bishop from among their ranks, Patriarch Yohanna Mārūn, or John Maron, thus became the first Patriarch of the Maronite Church in AD 685.

By this action, the Antiochene Syriac Maronite Church was formed, giving the Maronites a formal identity with theological clarity anchored in Chalcedonian Christology—a doctrine defined at the Council of Chalcedon in AD 451, asserting that Christ is one person in two distinct natures: fully divine and fully human. Naturally, Syriac was its liturgical language, reflecting Antiochene roots and heritage. Much to the dissatisfaction of Constantinople, shortly after, Yohanna Mārūn received support from Pope Sergius I, who himself hailed from an Antiochene family but was born in Sicily. This papal support created a Maronite-Greek schism. From this point onward, the Maronites maintained their contact with Rome, recognized as the "first among equals" of the five founding patriarchates—Rome, Alexandria, Antioch, Constantinople, and Jerusalem—of the original Christian Church. This constituted an early step in the eventual, formal and full, communion of the Maronite Church with Rome, which took place subsequently and gradually during the Crusades.

Patriarch Yohanna Mārūn, born in AD 628 in the ancient Greek city of Apamea, in the plains of the Orontes in today's Syria, led the Maronites through a difficult period of their history as well as a difficult period for Christianity and the Byzantine Empire. As a sign of a transition to come, Patriarch Yohanna Mārūn died in Lebanon in AD 707 and was buried in Kfarhay, a hill above the city of Batroun, Lebanon. Kfarhay was the first formal seat of the Maronite Patriarchate after moving it away from Antioch, following a very brief transitional period on the coast in the castle of Smar Jbeil.

Thus, subsequent to the Council of Chalcedon, the Church of Antioch went through a serious crisis that not only led to schisms but also to periods of vacancies in the Patriarchate seat as well as competing patriarchs. The prolonged patriarchal vacancies were due to fighting with the Muslim forces within the Empire as well as doctrinal bickering, leading to a major schism in AD 518. By then there were two patriarchal lines in Antioch: the Severus line, non-Chalcedonian—Syriac Orthodox; the Paul the Jew line, Chalcedonian—Greek Orthodox of Antioch, recognized as legitimate by the Byzantine authorities. A third line, also Chalcedonian, starting with Yohanna Mārūn in AD 686—Antiochene Syriac Maronite.

While doctrinal differences among the different factions in the Church of Antioch had been developing since AD 451, they reached their height in AD 512, when the Chalcedonian Patriarch, Flavian II, was replaced by the non-Chalcedonian Patriarch Severus at a synod held in the Phoenician city of Sidon. Unfortunately, the Church of Antioch—which had remained united under a single patriarchal line from its inception under Saint Peter in AD 34 through Severus' election in AD 512 and deposition in AD 518— split into three different patriarchal lines as result of accumulated differences. These are:

The Syriac Orthodox Patriarch of Antioch

The Syriac Orthodox Church of Antioch split from the original Church of Antioch after the deposition by the Byzantine authorities of Patriarch Severus in AD 518. This schism arose from Christological disagreements resulting from decisions made at the AD 451 Council of Chalcedon, which the Syriac Orthodox rejected and the Byzantine Emperor Justin I (AD 518-527) endorsed. As the last Patriarch of Antioch before the schism, Severus and his followers laid the foundations for a non-Chalcedonian, Syriac-speaking church—the Syriac Orthodox Church. The Syriac community endured persecution under both Byzantine and Arab rule, eventually relocating their Patriarchal seat from Antioch to Damascus.

The Greek Orthodox Patriarch of Antioch

After Severus' deposition, Paul the Jew was appointed Patriarch of the Chalcedonian faction of the Church of Antioch by the Byzantine Emperor, Justin I, in AD 518.

Given its close alliance with the Byzantines, this line became increasingly Greek in both liturgy and culture, reflecting the broader Hellenization of the church's leadership and laity, and eventually evolved into the Greek Orthodox Patriarchate of Antioch. The Greeks also faced political upheaval in Antioch and pressure by Arab forces. Today, this patriarchal seat is also headquartered in Damascus.

The Maronite Patriarch of Antioch

The Beit Mārūn community embraced Chalcedonian Christology and affiliated with the Greek Orthodox Church after the schism. Consequently, they faced attacks from the non-Chalcedonians. However, they also resented Byzantine control even though they were aligned in their struggle against the Arabs. Geographically isolated in Antioch and Mount Lebanon, the Maronites formally organized and elected their first Patriarch, Yohanna Mārūn, in AD 685, angering the Byzantine Emperor. Opposition from the Byzantine Empire to Yohanna Mārūn's election, combined with attacks from non-Chalcedonians in Antioch and the Arab conquests, drove more of the Maronites into Mount Lebanon, where they had already been asserting a distinct identity grounded in Monastic Syriac liturgy.

Maronite Transition from Antioch to Mount Lebanon—The Making of a New Homeland

Life for the Maronites on the Orontes was getting even more dangerous. In AD 694, the Byzantine ruler, Justinian II (AD 685-695 and AD 705-711), in a deal with the Umayyads, ordered an attack on the Maronites, destroying their monasteries and killing many of their clergy. This was on the heels of hostilities they perpetrated against the Maronites, and other Christians, in Mount Lebanon, where they already had a significant presence and were actively resisting Arab rule. A defining moment was the Battle of Amioun, in the northern part of Mount Lebanon, in AD 694, when the Christian communities, especially the Maronites, who were led by their Patriarch in-person, fought both the Byzantines and the Arabs, resisted and emerged victorious. However, they also understood that their freedom and survival had become paramount, and there was a heavy price for them to pay to save and maintain their precious autonomy in what had been, up until this point, a peaceful and serene mountain.

By the end of the seventh century, the distinct Christian community originally created by Saint Maron in his birthplace of Antioch already had a counterpart thriving in Lebanon. Feeling increasingly isolated from other Christians in the Byzantine Empire, the Maronites began to distance themselves from their original roots in Antioch and began to join another community that also shared their language and beliefs in Mount Lebanon.

In parallel, the Muslim march approaching Anatolia created an urgency and further accelerated the Maronites' migration from Antioch to Lebanon, where they could join together with other Christians, united in their defense of a shared faith. Thus, starting at the mouth of the Orontes River on the Mediterranean Sea and its surrounding area in Antioch, following the natural flow of the river all the way to its source in Lebanon, they set out on their journey, initially settling in Hermel, in Lebanon's Beqaa Valley. From there, the arriving Maronites dispersed and made a home for themselves among other Christians in and around the Mount Lebanon areas of Bsharri and Mnaitra, toiling in the fields and rugged mountains under the cedars of Lebanon in order to make their living, fortifying their sanctuaries, and building their churches in the hills and valleys of Qannoubine and Qadisha to preserve their faith. Subsequently, the Maronites scattered further into much of the original territories of Mount Lebanon and integrated with the existing Christian population, including fellow Maronites, eventually reaching all corners of the country.

The Orontes River from its Source in Lebanon to its Mouth in Türkiye Traversing Northern Syria

Furthermore, Phoenicia was itself seeing a two-path growth in its Christian community, with the coastal cities embracing a Greek and Byzantine culture and the mountains, insulated from the outside world by their harsh terrain and weather, embracing the Syriac culture. During the same time, Northern and Central Phoenicia was attracting, from other parts of the Byzantine Empire, Melkite Christians whose theology and language of their liturgy were influenced by the Greek Christian theology of Constantinople. Over time, a coherent national and religious identity began to emerge in Mount Lebanon and the rest of Phoenicia, which eventually gave way to the name "Lebanon" for the entire territory.

The seventh century AD was an eventful one for the Byzantine Empire, but most serious was the challenge it faced from the Arabian Peninsula. While the Eastern Empire survived for a thousand years after the fall of its western half, ending in AD 1453, its role in Lebanon and the Levant severely diminished subsequent to the death of the Prophet Muhammad in AD 632. In AD 636, Lebanon's plains, but not its mountains, were fully conquered by the Arab Muslim forces advancing westward as were many major cities in other parts of the Empire. Very swiftly, mass conversions were taking place in various locations controlled by the Arabs. However, that was not the case in Lebanon, especially in the mountains.

At the start of the Muslim conquests, as Arab forces moved swiftly across the Levant—including westward toward Jerusalem and, by proximity and cultural connection, into what is now Lebanon—the Christian communities of the region found themselves at a critical crossroads in how to respond to unfolding events. Many, especially those in, or having access to, the Mount Lebanon range, opted to settle into the rugged mountains and guard their traditions. There, for centuries, they demonstrated remarkable resilience, adaptability, and self-sufficiency, sustaining a way of life under harsh conditions. This mountain refuge became a symbol of endurance, rooted in both faith and connection to the land.

Perhaps the strong Phoenician connection to Christianity can explain why the Christians in Lebanon, the heartland of Phoenicia, remained so steadfast in their beliefs despite Christianity's eventual decline in other surrounding lands. I believe this formative experience, and others like it throughout Lebanon's long and often turbulent history, helps explain why the Lebanese people have continually managed to endure, rebuild, and carry on despite centuries of conflict and recurring hardship. This legacy of tenacity and spiritual conviction, forged in isolation, remains a defining trait of the Lebanese character today.

PART TWO

From the Arab Conquests to the Crusades

CHAPTER 5.

The Arab Conquests and the Spread of Islam

IN THE SEVENTH CENTURY, a new religion, Islam, emerged in the city of Mecca on the Arabian Peninsula, presenting the Byzantine Empire with a serious challenge and ultimately a fatal blow. The Prophet of Islam, Muhammad, received his first revelation in 610, and such revelations continued until his death in 632. Collectively, these verbal messages, which the Prophet received from God through the angel Gabriel, became the Quran. Muhammad readily shared these messages with people in his immediate surroundings, initially in the city of Mecca and subsequently in the city of Medina, constituting the formal establishment of the religion.

The Prophet Muhammad first shared these messages of faith with his wife Khadija, then his closest family members, and next with trusted friends. However, his message was not accepted by others within his community, and he soon had to leave Mecca, his home city, for another city, Medina, in order to escape persecution. In Medina, he was able to practice his new religion and build a following for Islam. He returned to Mecca in 629 and worked to convert the people of Arabia to the new faith.

The Prophet died two years after his return to Mecca. Within a short period of time after his death, around 632, the Prophet's followers began to dutifully spread their religion in all directions by conquering other lands and converting their inhabitants. As a core tenet of the faith, he encouraged his followers to spread the message of Islam to the wider community. In fact, multiple surahs, or chapters, in the Quran emphasize the importance of *da'wah*, the spreading of Islam's message. Thus, Arab Muslims launched a series of conquests, with ideological and military intent: to seize new territories and to spread the new religion near and far, in the Byzantine Empire and beyond.

The Impact of Islam on the Byzantine Empire and Lebanon

It did not take long before Jerusalem, under the rule of the Byzantines at the time, capitulated to an armed invasion in 636. Surrounding territories in the Levant, evidently less fortified, soon followed suit, and their Christian, Jewish, and polytheist populations were commanded to convert. A large Muslim empire spanning three different continents, Asia, Africa, and Europe, was quickly created. By 640, much of the Levant, including Lebanon, had fallen to advancing Muslim forces.

The Canaanites, conquered by many empires throughout their history, were able to hold onto their beliefs under every civilization that ruled them primarily because of commonalities among polytheism, the religion of most of these invaders at that time. However, they explicitly chose and were able to freely adopt Christianity as a new religion for themselves, starting in the first century after the death of Christ, under one of the most oppressive conquerors, the Roman Empire, who were also polytheists and initially opposed Christianity before it spread throughout their empire. Many Canaanites became Christians under Roman rule long before the Roman Empire adopted Christianity.

In the seventh century, a different situation emerged when, for the first time, neither choice nor freedom were options. However, while the Quran called for Muslims to fight non-believers, it also gave those who could afford it, the option to pay a tax, the *Jizya*, in order to receive protection from their Muslim rulers. This time, the Lebanese, and their neighbors, encountered a ruler with an explicit policy of promulgating a new religion, language, and culture in place of the prevailing religions and languages in the Levant.

Not everyone was prepared to quickly accept the terms of the new ruler. Some Christian communities, like those in Lebanon, put up a fierce fight in defense of their freedom, religious beliefs, and way of life, retreating into the hinterland, where they were able to fortify their rugged terrains and resist. The Maronites, one of the prominent Christian communities in Mount Lebanon that had before sought refuge in the mountains of Lebanon, and now increasingly so to avoid coming under Muslim rule during the Arab conquests, worked to mend their relationship with the remnants of the Byzantine Empire. Having distanced themselves from direct contact with them earlier, this rapprochement provided the Christians with political and military support that enabled them to launch counterattacks on Arab forces outside their territories, thus giving relief and protection to themselves but also other beleaguered Christians throughout the Levant.

Because of its relative isolation and independence throughout these periods of foreign rule, Mount Lebanon continued to be a safe haven for Christians and other religious minorities fleeing persecution in nearby lands. The rugged terrain of the Lebanese mountains, their harsh winter weather, and, most notably, the valiant nature of their inhabitants proved to be a real challenge for the advancing forces who hailed from a desert landscape and climate and therefore were not accustomed to living conditions in such an environment.

Like other conquerors before them, the Arabs, initially localized in the Arabian Peninsula, set out to gain control and influence beyond their boundaries. However, their desire to conquer other lands was motivated primarily by their religious call. Their *jihad*, or struggle, defeated the Byzantines and brought Islam to

Lebanon very early, in 636, but they were capable of fully capturing only coastal lands. While the Lebanese mountains were always surrounded, the Christians living there were deprived of certain freedoms and therefore resisted, and were able to retain a degree of autonomy, depending on the rulers and circumstances. Where the local population in Lebanon rejected conversion to Islam, the Caliphates resorted to bringing and stationing people from their own and other conquered regions to subdue and defend land they occupied. The waves of organized migration into Lebanon continued through the last Caliphate. These newcomers eventually settled in the areas they came to, living side by side with those who came before them as well as the original inhabitants. Successive Muslim dynasties ruled Lebanon until the end of the First World War when the last of these empires, the Ottoman, was defeated in 1918. The end of this war led to significant geopolitical changes and a new set of challenges, as the region was divided up by European powers, and its borders were redrawn under the terms of the 1916 Sykes-Picot Agreement and the 1917 Balfour Declaration.

The Sunni-Shia Schism

After the Prophet Muhammad's death, his close associate and friend, Abu Bakr, was selected as the first Caliph to lead the followers of Islam, as a successor to the Prophet. Some Muslims believed that Abu Bakr was the proper successor because he was the closest confidant to the Prophet. However, other Muslims believed that lineage should be the deciding factor. Thus, Ali Ibn Abi Talib should be the successor because he was a cousin and son-in-law of Muhammad. This caused an immediate war lasting through the reign of subsequent Caliphates and a major schism in Islam, with ramifications into the present time. Those that believed the Caliph should be an elected leader of the faith became known as Sunni; they are the majority in Islam and have always had the upper hand. Those that believed the Caliph should be selected based on family lineage became known as Shia; they are the minority in Islam. At the center of this dispute was Ali's supporters who believed that God, through the Prophet Muhammad, appointed Ali to be spiritual and political successor to the Prophet as first of twelve Imams that will be in the succession line. The twelfth and final Imam will be in a state of occultation until he reappears again at an unknown time, bringing justice and peace to the world. This branch of Islam subsequently became known as the Twelvers.

Under Muslim rule of the Levant, other non-Sunni Muslim minorities flocked to Mount Lebanon in search of religious freedom. As early as the seventh century, supporters of Ali Ibn Abi Talib migrated from the Arabian Peninsula, and later from Egypt to Mount Lebanon and the Beqaa region, and subsequently into South Lebanon. The treatment of Shia in Lebanon under various Muslim Caliphates varied significantly and depended on the ruling dynasty and its sectarian orientation. The mountains of Jbeil and Keserwan, the Beqaa, and Jabal Amel were instrumental in providing the Shia a natural refuge from external pressures. Also, many of the descendants of the Muwahhidun, or Druze, now living in Lebanon, fled persecution in Egypt and found a refuge in Mount Lebanon. At the time the Druze were an offshoot of a Shia group that subsequently adopted their new religion.

The Marada Resistance in Mount Lebanon

Replacing the Byzantines, Lebanon was ruled by successive Muslim Caliphates, or dynasties, until the end of the First World War. Neither the initial battles to control Lebanon nor the subsequent efforts to maintain control over the conquered land were painless for the conquerors. The Christian inhabitants of Mount Lebanon, and especially the Maronites, fought back to secure their homeland and preserve their beliefs. There is an important point to make here relating to the origin and background of one of these rebellious groups of Christian people, often referred to as the Mardaites, or simply Marada. The Marada were present in the Levantine mountains from Antioch to Galilee at the time of the Arab Conquests, living in Mount Lebanon harmoniously side-by-side with other Christians, including the Maronites. Their mountainous geography afforded them natural defenses that enabled them to protect their independence, fiercely refusing to fully submit either religiously or politically.

There are a number of questions that often arise regarding the Marada, including whether they are the same people as the Jarajima and, more importantly, what exactly their relationship is to the Maronites. In general, historians agree that the Marada and Jarajima are the same people but offer different and conflicting answers to the question of their relation to the Maronites. However, some things are not in dispute, and these are the documented bravery of the Marada in repelling attacks on the mountains, their common Syriac language, and their Christian faith.

The more difficult question than who are the Marada is whether they are the ancestors of the Maronites, or whether they are simply two geographically and religiously related groups of people who merged into one as they, and other natives of the mountains, worked to defend themselves against a common threat. Although there is evidence that the Marada originated from the ancient Amanus mountains, now called Nur Mountains, a range located along the Cilician-Syrian border, within Türkiye's Hatay Province, historians have offered a number of possibilities for their ethnicity, most often Persian and Greek, and sometimes Armenian.

The greatest certainty is that they indeed existed. The first written mention of the Marada was by Saint Theophanes the Confessor, a Byzantine aristocrat who served in the court of Emperor Leo IV (775-780), prior to becoming a Christian monk. He wrote that toward the end of the seventh century, the Marada controlled mountains and land in Lebanon reaching the Galilee, in addition to their own stronghold of the Amanus mountains.

More important and recognized is that their coordinated resistance contributed to the survival and preservation of Christian faith in Lebanon under centuries of foreign rule. This resistance also became a symbol of struggle and survival for other Christians in the Levant. However, despite the resistance, in the end, Lebanon was integrated into the Caliphates, and the Christians of Lebanon lived under the conditions of their rulers, including being given *dhimmi* status as "People of the Book," according to Islamic legal code. The same status was extended to Jewish populations in Lebanon and throughout the Levant. This afforded them some protection in return for paying the *jizya*, which was often beyond the average person's affordability.

Despite being vastly outnumbered and facing the military might of advancing Arab forces during the early Islamic conquests and subsequent periods, the inhabitants of the Lebanese mountains engaged in intermittent, localized resistance rather than a continuous, unified defense. Their rugged terrain, strong local leadership, and cohesive communal identities enabled them to preserve a degree of autonomy that would define the region's historical character for centuries. This complex pattern of resistance not only shaped Lebanon's political and religious landscape but also laid the foundations for the unique communal balance that continues to define the country's modern identity.

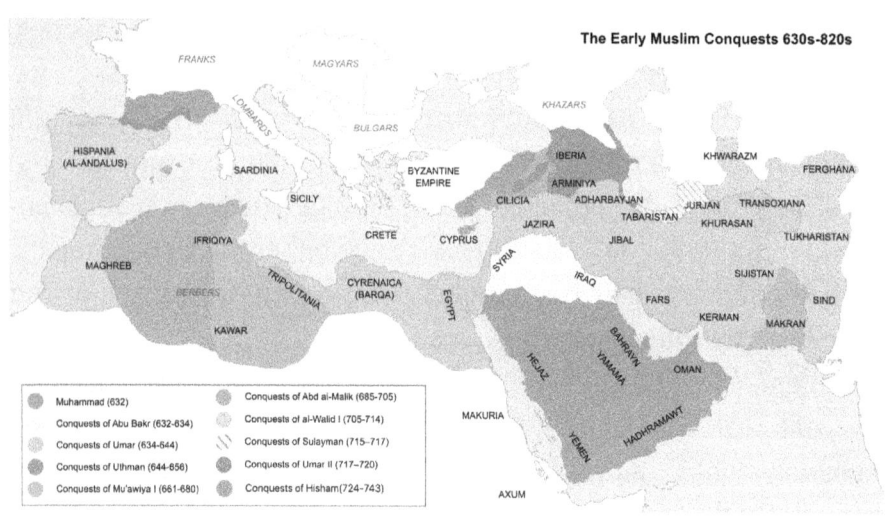

The Early Muslim Conquests

CHAPTER 6.

Muslim Caliphates and Dynasties in Lebanon

THE POLITICAL-RELIGIOUS STATE COMPRISING THE acquired lands and the Muslim community within, as well as the original inhabitants of these lands living under Muslim rule, were governed by a succession of Muslim Caliphates and dynasties from 632 to 1918. Entities considered to wield not only political and military authority but also religious authority over the broader Muslim community are formally recognized as Caliphates. These Caliphates were theocracies headed by a dual, religious and political, supreme leader, usually referred to as a Caliph, who is regarded as the successor to the Prophet Muhammad. In contrast, dynasties generally claimed political and military authority but did not claim universal spiritual leadership, thus were not considered Caliphates. At times, the reign of some Caliphates also overlapped with the reign of some competing dynasties.

The different Caliphates and dynasties were the Rashidun Caliphate (632-661), the Umayyad Caliphate (661-750), the Abbasid Caliphate (750-1258), the Fatimid Caliphate (909-1171), the Seljuks (1037-1308), the Ayyubids (1171-1260), the Mamluks (1261-1517), and the Ottoman Caliphate (1299-1918). Even though their impact on Lebanon was somewhat limited, the Seljuks and Ayyubids had a special focus on Jerusalem, which makes them a subject of interest given the geographic proximity of Jerusalem to Lebanon. In addition, there were several other overlapping dynasties during much of the Arab and Muslim rule, some of significance and other smaller ones, representing different competing clans, tribes, and nations. Because these were mainly localized, they are not relevant to Lebanon and thus are not discussed here.

Also, the Jewish communities of the Levant, including Lebanon, were still visible during this time, playing a significant role in the broader sociopolitical and economic dynamics of the region. Under the Muslim Caliphates and dynasties, starting with the Rashiduns and through the Ottomans, Jewish communities generally experienced a mix of protection and religious restrictions. Like Christians, as "People of the Book," or *dhimmis*, they were allowed to practice their religion within the framework of Islamic rule, in exchange for paying the *jizya*. Jewish communities living in Lebanon's coastal cities, such as Beirut, Tyre, and Sidon, thrived economically and culturally, contributing to trade, finance, craftsmanship, and intellectual life. They also often acted as intermediaries between different religious and ethnic groups, facilitating economic activities across Muslim, Christian, and Jewish communities. However, also similar to Christians, during times of religious tension, Jews faced persecution and forced conversions. Overall, under the various Islamic Caliphates, Jewish communities were generally able to maintain their own distinct cultural, religious, and social identities, although they had to adapt continuously to changing religious and political environments.

To understand the complex social fabric of modern Lebanon, it is essential to examine the long historical legacy of Arab and Muslim rule in the country and the broader region. Over more than a millennium, successive Islamic regimes—from the Rashidun Caliphate to the Ottoman Caliphate—shaped Lebanon's religious diversity, the political autonomy of its mountainous communities, and lasting sectarian structures. As well, Seljuks and the Ayyubids, both Sunni Muslim dynasties, played militaristic roles as the first non-Arab Muslim dynasty to rise to power. This legacy must be viewed alongside other major historical forces, including colonialism, emergent nationalism, and shifting global geopolitics.

The Rashidun Caliphate

The Rashidun Caliphate (632-661) was essentially the First Islamic State. Its capital was Medina, in today's Saudi Arabia. Up until the Prophet Muhammad's death, Islam was limited to the Arabian Peninsula. The Rashiduns led the early Arab conquests that expanded Islam's reach and presence beyond its original boundaries. The Rashiduns, which means the "Rightly Guided," were the first four Caliphs who succeeded the Prophet in ruling over Islam. In fact, they all knew him well and had been trusted associates and close relations. They were Abu Bakr Abdullah, the father of Aisha, a wife of the Prophet, and his trusted advisor; Umar ibn al-Khattab, father of Hafsa, a wife of the Prophet, and also his close associate; Uthman ibn Affan, a son-in-law of the Prophet and a second cousin; and Ali ibn Abi Talib, a son-in-law of the Prophet and a cousin. Although Imam Ali was not selected as the rightful first successor to the Prophet Muhammad, as his family and supporters had wished, he is considered as the first Imam in Shia Islam. In Sunni Islam, Ali ibn Abi Talib is recognized as the fourth Caliph of the Rashidun, a position of considerable religious and political significance.

During the Rashidun Caliphate, Muslim forces, stationed throughout the Lebanese coast, exerted influence toward converting residents to Islam, although many resisted. Also, hunkered down in their mountain strongholds, the Maronites and other Christians held to their faiths and traditions. However, while the Christian community in the mountains was able to remain safe and maintain some autonomy, they, as well as Christians elsewhere in

Lebanon, were obliged to pay the *jizya* to Islamic rulers, especially to avoid military service.

Not knowing what lay ahead, the Christians also mobilized to protect their faith and identity by moving into even more remote and rugged places, setting out to transform some of the most difficult landscapes into self-sustaining farmland for their growing community. Similarly, the strengthening of religious institutions, including churches, monasteries, and schools, was intensified throughout the mountains and other locations in Lebanon. Thus, a stronghold for daily survival and spiritual needs was brought forth in the heart of Lebanon.

Naturally, the presence of a Sunni Muslim community in Lebanon is traced to this period. In fact, conversions to Islam took place as early as the arrival of the Rashiduns. These conversions were more common in coastal cities. While conversions continued with succeeding Caliphates, waves of Sunni Muslim migration into Lebanon also followed. This migration was interrupted during certain periods as Caliphates changed hands, for example under the Fatimids. Additional waves of Sunni migration, particularly to Beirut and North Lebanon, resumed after the Fatimids through the last Caliphate.

While the Rashiduns did not actively persecute Shia, who were not yet present in Lebanon, they were marginalized elsewhere in the early days of the Caliphate and beyond, except for certain periods, and felt a sense of resentment for not succeeding in choosing Ali ibn Abi Talib as the first successor to the Prophet Muhammad.

Living in major Lebanese cities, where they had a long-established presence, members of the Jewish community were heavily involved in the Mediterranean economic network, trading goods between the Levant, Europe, and North Africa. They were particularly influential in the silk commerce and textile manufacturing. Under the Rashidun Caliphate, Jewish people continued to engage in commerce and, as *dhimmis*, were protected but subjected to the *jizya* and certain legal restrictions. While they were allowed to practice their religion with restrictions, they remained a marginalized group in the broader social and political hierarchy. To preserve their ancient Jewish knowledge, they engaged in efforts to produce texts in Hebrew and Aramaic, as well Arabic, a new language to coastal Lebanon.

The Umayyad Caliphate

The Umayyad Caliphate (661-750), the second Islamic state after the death of the Prophet Muhammad, continued the conquests beyond the Byzantine Empire in Asia, Africa, and Europe, ruling over a vast territory and population that, by then, was primarily Christian. In fact, the Umayyad's territory was the largest, by land mass, among all Caliphates. As per Islamic law, those who did not convert to Islam had to pay the *jizya* in order to continue the practice of their religion under relative autonomy. In addition, the Umayyads introduced a compulsory enforcement of the Arabic language on their subjects, most of whom did not speak it. With Damascus becoming the capital for the Umayyads, the coastal cities as well as parts of Mount Lebanon were easily ruled by the Umayyads. The Umayyads also established the inland Lebanese city of Anjar as a major trade hub and a link between their capital and the plains of the Levant.

Under the Umayyad reign, more Muslims were settled on the Lebanese coast seemingly to assist in fending off naval Byzantine attacks. From time to time, the Christians were able to exploit the ongoing war between the two factions of Islam in their own favor by siding with the Sunni Umayyads. However, the Umayyads still had to fend off raids by the Marada and Maronites, who guarded their sacred strongholds in the Lebanese mountains, sometimes by fighting back and at other times by offering them incentives. Ironically, despite earlier political differences and animosities between the Byzantines and the Maronites in Antioch that eventually led to their separation, Emperor Constantine IV (668-685), the ruler of the Byzantine Empire during this period, offered the Christians, including the Maronites, political and military support. In fact, Christian hard-fought incursions against the Umayyads caused them significant harm, requiring the Umayyad Caliph to reach an autonomy agreement with the Marada and a financial agreement with the Byzantine rulers in return for cessation of attacks. Such agreements with Byzantine rulers, at times, became detrimental to the Christians in Mount Lebanon because they resulted in being pressured into disarming or relocating out of the mountains and into other Byzantine territories.

The Shia communities in the Umayyad Caliphate faced discrimination. To escape persecution, supporters of Ali ibn Abi Talib from various parts of the Caliphate also began to seek refuge in the rugged mountain areas of Lebanon. The Umayyads, however, became particularly harsh toward the Shia they encountered in Lebanon.

Members of the Jewish community were considered *dhimmis* and paid the *jizya*. They practiced their religion, also with restrictions, and were relegated to the margins of society.

The Abbasid Caliphate

When the Abbasid Caliphate (750-1258) came to power, defeating the Umayyads, they also took control of Lebanon, ruling from Baghdad as their capital. The policy of allowing Christians to practice their religion provided they paid their *jizya*, as was the case under earlier Islamic Caliphates, was continued. Also, as with earlier Caliphates, the Christians fought to keep some form of autonomy for themselves, despite the risk of retribution. Early on, in 752, the Christians and others in Mount Lebanon and on the coast, staged repeated revolts against the Abbasids' oppressive treatment and harsh taxation. Two noted revolts: the first, originating in Baskinta and eventually centered in the area of the Beqaa Valley;

and the second, starting in the Mnaitra and spreading toward the Baalbek area. Also, during this period under the fourth Maronite Patriarch, Yohanna Mārūn II, the patriarchal residence was moved from Kfarhay, a hill that was relatively close to the coast of Batroun, where Muslim control was strong, to their monastery in Yanouh, Jbeil, high above the sea into the relative safety of the mountains. This pattern of relocating the seat of the Maronite Patriarchate, higher into the mountains or deeper in the valleys, in search of safer grounds persisted by moving next into the Our Lady of Ilige, or Elige, Monastery in Mayfouk, also in the district of Jbeil; then Qannoubine, in the Qadisha Valley, and Dimane, overlooking the Valley, among other locations, before Bkerké finally became the permanent patriarchal seat toward the end of the 19th century. Moreover, more Christians continued to migrate into Mount Lebanon, particularly Maronites, as they already were coming to terms with the idea that their presence in Lebanon was essentially their permanent homeland, especially after a final devastating attack in 936 on what was left of Beit Mārūn and the other Maronite monasteries in Antioch facing the same fate, or beyond reach.

Starting in the early parts of this era, members originally of Northern Arabian tribes began migrating to Lebanon, including the Aley and Chouf mountains above Beirut, eventually becoming a prominent community in Lebanon. Soon, two noted groups, the Lakhmids and the Tanukhids, were tasked by the Abbasids with guarding the Lebanese coast against the Byzantines, and did so under the subsequent Caliphates of Fatimids, Ayyubids, and Mamluks. Before arriving in Lebanon, the Lakhmids and Tanukhids had embraced Islam as Ismaili Shia under an Abbasid Caliph in Egypt. The Ismailis are the second-largest group, after the Twelvers, within the Shia branch of Islam. They split from the Twelvers group in 765 after a dispute over the selection of the seventh Imam. The Ismailli Shia are led by an Imam with direct lineage of Imam Ali, the cousin and son-in-law of Prophet Muhammad, and Fatima, the daughter of Muhammad.

*Author at the Monastery of Saint John Maron,
First Patriarchal Residence at Kfarhay*

***Author at the Monastery of Our Lady of Ilige,
Patriarchal Residence at Mayfouk***

Starting in the early parts of this era, members originally of Northern Arabian tribes began migrating to Lebanon, including the Aley and Chouf mountains above Beirut, eventually becoming a prominent community in Lebanon. Soon, two noted groups, the Lakhmids and the Tanukhids, were tasked by the Abbasids with guarding the Lebanese coast against the Byzantines, and did so under the subsequent Caliphates of Fatimids, Ayyubids, and Mamluks. Before arriving in Lebanon, the Lakhmids and Tanukhids had embraced Islam as Ismaili Shia under an Abbasid

Caliph in Egypt. The Ismailis are the second-largest group, after the Twelvers, within the Shia branch of Islam. They split from the Twelvers group in 765 after a dispute over the selection of the seventh Imam. The Ismailli Shia are led by an Imam with direct lineage of Imam Ali, the cousin and son-in-law of Prophet Muhammad, and Fatima, the daughter of Muhammad.

Centuries before this, along with the originally Southern Arabian Ghassanid tribe, they were Christian. The Ghassanid tribe had migrated to the Levant in the third century and established a strong Christian presence there. This would soon change again for the Lakhmids and the Tanukhids. In the 1020s, they diverged from Ismaili Shia Islam and adopted the Druze faith, and were subsequently given feudal fiefdoms by the Caliphates for their cooperation. Shortly after, in the 12th century, members of the Southern Arabian Qahtani tribe, the Banu Maan, originally from Yemen, also arrived in Lebanon and joined the existing Druze community. The Maans became a prominent group that also ruled Mount Lebanon in a later period. However, for the first time, this Caliphate realized that it could exploit the emergent religious diversity of Mount Lebanon, using what became a common and lasting policy of "divide and conquer" over the Lebanese population by their occupiers of the time. Such a policy was also used by the Abbasids in other areas under their control.

Several Shia uprisings in Lebanon during the Abbasid period, often centered around claims of Ali ibn Abi Talib's descendants, led to crackdowns on their communities and contributed to further marginalization.

The Jewish community continued to live under the same *dhimmi* status—marginalized and subject to the *jizya*, as they did under the Rashidun and Umayyad Caliphates. However, they benefited from the relative cultural tolerance of the Abbasid period, during which Jewish scholars made significant contributions to Arabic literature, medicine, and philosophy. Also, they were often involved in translating Greek and Persian texts into Arabic, facilitating the transmission of classical knowledge.

The Fatimid Caliphate

Lebanon fell under the dominance of the Fatimid Caliphate (909-1171) toward the end of the 10th century, around 969, overlapping and challenging the Sunni Abbasid Caliphate from their new Cairo capital. Although the Fatimid rulers held the title of Caliph, as a Shia dynasty, their Caliphate was considered separate from the earlier three Sunni Caliphates of the Rashidun, Umayyad, and Abbasid.

The Fatimids, descendants from the Prophet Muhammad through his daughter Fatimah and her husband, Imam Ali ibn Abi Talib, were adherents of Ismaili Shia. This resulted in two Caliphates operating at the same time, in different places, vying for legitimacy and power. The Fatimids controlled all coastal cities, including Tripoli, Beirut, Sidon, and Tyre, where they settled more incoming Shia. As the influx of more Christians continued into Mount Lebanon, Fatimid rulers were tightening their grip on the coastal cities, using their might and the mercenaries they brought in from other areas they conquered.

Given their animosity with the Sunnis, the Fatimid showed some acceptance to Christians and other minorities under their rule. At the same time, they were also challenging Christian autonomy in the mountains, strengthening taxation on them, and playing on religious fault lines, as they prepared to defend against the emerging European plans to recapture the Holy Land from Muslims. By now, living side by side, the Christians and their new neighbors, the Druze, for the most part, coexisted peacefully in the mountains, although violent clashes would erupt periodically.

The Fatimids provided a period of relief for the Shia in Lebanon, especially as more arrived seeking safety and protection. They actively promoted Shia Islam, particularly their Ismaili branch. In fact, this period also saw the spread of Ismailism in various areas of Lebanon, although their numbers remained small. However, the large number of Banu Amila, originally a Yemeni tribe that settled in South Lebanon, belong to the main branch of Shia Islam, the Twelvers. The Shia eventually became the dominant group in the Beqaa Valley and Southern Lebanon, particularly the area around Tyre, prompting the naming of the region as Jabal Amel, in reference to Banu Amila. During this period, Shia communities throughout Lebanon, especially Jabal Amel as it became the main center of Shia settlement, experienced greater freedom and practiced their faith openly.

Under the Fatimids, Jewish people retained their *dhimmi* status but experienced relative prosperity. Consistent with the Fatimids' generally tolerant approach toward non-Muslims, they granted the Jewish community more freedom in practicing their religion in synagogues. They were also allowed to maintain their own religious schools, communal leadership, and systems of self-governance.

The Seljuks

The Seljuks (1037-1308) were a Sunni Muslim dynasty with roots originating from a Turkic tribe in Central Asia, challenging both Abbasids and Fatimids. They were the first non-Arab Muslim dynasty to rise to power. They began as mercenaries for the Abbasids but assumed full power from them in Baghdad in 1055. Despite their political dominance, the Seljuks continued to acknowledge the Abbasid Caliph as the spiritual authority of the Muslim world.

The Seljuks brought their culture and Islam to Anatolia. Despite their control of massive territories, including in the Levant, they had little influence on Lebanon, which was under the control of other Muslim dynasties and the Crusaders during this period. Even though the Seljuks did not fully rule Lebanon, their control of the important swath of land from Persia to Jerusalem impacted much of the Levant, including Lebanon, and certainly all of Antioch. In

1071, the Seljuks conquered Jerusalem, which stayed under their rule for nearly a quarter of a century. Shortly after, a rebellion in Jerusalem ejected them from the city. However, the Seljuk army managed to lay siege to Jerusalem again, retaking it while causing much killing, destruction, and looting. The Seljuks and the Fatimids battled over Jerusalem, taking turns occupying it. As a result, non-Muslim residents of the city suffered systematic persecution until the Seljuks received their final defeat at the hand of the Crusaders in their first war, in 1099, when they freed Jerusalem and the rest of the Holy Land. With this, the 500-year Islamic rule of Jerusalem came to an end. This would later change again.

Even though the Seljuks were marginally present in Lebanon, the Shia there faced renewed discrimination during the Seljuks period, leading them to continue to consolidate their communities in more remote areas.

The Jewish community had a complex relationship with the Seljuks. As *dhimmis*, they paid the *jizya* but faced restrictions, including prohibitions on building new synagogues larger than existing ones and being confined to specific neighborhoods or quarters within cities. Despite these limitations, the Seljuks engaged Jewish merchants to serve as intermediaries in facilitating commerce between the Muslim world and Europe, leveraging their established commercial networks across the Mediterranean.

The Ayyubids

The Ayyubids (1171-1260), a Sunni Muslim dynasty, was established by Kurdish Zangid Salah al-Din, or Saladin, after defeating the Fatimid Caliphate in Egypt. Their initial capital was Cairo, but it was subsequently moved to Damascus and then to Aleppo. They did not claim the title of Caliph and, primarily, ruled Egypt and Syria but also held other territories in Arabia including Iraq and Yemen. One of the major battles won by the Ayyubids under General Saladin against the Crusaders' Kingdom of Jerusalem took place in 1179 in Marjaayoun, Lebanon. The Ayyubids did not fully rule Lebanon; it was under the Crusaders' control at that time. However, Beirut and Sidon fell to Saladin as they captured Jerusalem and other territories held by the Crusaders in 1187. In 1229, under the Treaty of Jaffa, the Ayyubids ceded Jerusalem back to the Crusaders, who controlled the city until 1244, when the Ayyubids reclaimed it. Saladin's war against the Crusaders severely weakened their ability to defend themselves and the land they held, giving Muslims the upper hand again in the Holy Land and tight control over Jerusalem as well as many other important cities nearby. The Ayyubids employed enslaved warriors to help them in their military expeditions. These indentured soldiers would eventually overthrow the Ayyubids, becoming the Mamluk dynasty themselves.

The Ayyubids actively suppressed and marginalized the Shia population, including efforts to convert them into Sunnis. Furthermore, despite their limited presence in Lebanon, the Ayyubids, at that time, managed to establish a presence for a small Kurdish community in Lebanon.

The Ayyubid period was marked by relative prosperity and tolerance for the Jewish community in Lebanon. They were able to continue their religious and social practices, even though they were still subject to the *dhimmi* status and *jizya*. Also, they were able to engage in their commercial and trade activities. However, Jewish schools and synagogues operated in their community with some restrictions.

Up until this point, except for their interactions with others within their protected sphere and the obligatory, but distrustful, dealings with their successive regimes, the Christians in Lebanon had been in self-imposed seclusion since the arrival of the first Caliphate, nearly five centuries before. By this time, under Arab and Muslim rule, Islam—as well as the Arabic language and culture—became widespread in Lebanon. While Islam became the majority religion in the broader region, Christianity remained predominant within Lebanon. This altered demographic and cultural landscape in the country is foundational to Lebanon's rich and enduring religious mosaic.

CHAPTER 7.

The Great Christian Schism

THE ROMAN EMPEROR CONSTANTINE (306-337) can be credited with two important developments in the history of Christendom. First, and in many ways directly, is the wide acceptance of Christianity in his new territory, the Byzantine Empire; and second, but indirectly, is the eventual division of the territory along East–West lines. Constantine's decision to establish a new capital for his new Roman Empire, away from Rome, on the site of the renamed Greek city of Byzantium, Constantinople, was not a random act. Rome's association with polytheism, despite it being the seat of the Christian Pope, made it inappropriate to be the center of the Christian Empire he envisioned. More than seven centuries after this, the city of Constantinople played a decisive role in the Great East–West Schism of 1054, a persistent division of the Christian Church. This Schism and the earlier schisms within the Church of Antioch have impacted Lebanon, eventually resulting in the presence of all denominations and sects of Christianity stemming from these schisms in the country, making it an important topic to carefully consider and understand if we are to conceptualize the history of Christianity in Lebanon.

Context

The Great Schism split the Christian Church into the Eastern Orthodox and the Roman Catholic churches. Theological and organizational differences between the Eastern and Western sides of the Church arose almost from the onset of Christianity. The divergent lingual, cultural, and political identity of Christians in the East and West shaped the different churches they eventually became. One of the theological differences that caused a schism among the Christians in the East, subsequent to the Ecumenical Council of Chalcedon of 451, and continued to linger, was the "*Filioque,*" or "*...and the Son*" in the Creed. The original text of the Creed, accepted at the Council of Nicaea in 325, stated that the Holy Spirit proceeds only from the Father. However, the Western Church added this phrase indicating that the Holy Spirit proceeds from both the Father and the Son. Many from the Eastern Church rejected this change, arguing that it was an unauthorized alteration of the Creed and a misrepresentation of the relationship within the Holy Trinity.

Another tension-causing difference relates to the authority of the Pope, the Patriarch of the West. The Pope demanded supremacy over the other four patriarchs, based on the notion that Saint Peter, as the first Pope, had a special standing in the Church. The Eastern Church did not agree to this and favored a conciliar model, in which authority was shared among all the patriarchs and bishops. In 1054, these differences, most prominent between the Church of Rome and the Church of Constantinople, seemingly over papal authority but also over lingering Christological disputes, led to a total break in the communion between East and West. This stalemate, becoming known as the Great Schism, resulted in two divergent churches, one known as Catholic and the other known as Orthodox.

A clarification regarding these two terms is warranted at this time. The word "catholic" means "universal" or "all-encompassing," for example, in referring broadly to all believers in Jesus Christ. The word "orthodox" means "correct," "true," or "conforming," for example in referring to creeds that cannot be changed. The first recorded use of the word "catholic" was by Ignatius of Antioch, the second Bishop of Antioch, after Saint Peter. About the year 110, he wrote in the *Epistle to the Smyrnaeans*: "*You must all follow the bishop as Jesus Christ follows the Father, and the presbytery as you would the apostles. Wherever the bishop appears, let the people be there; just as wherever Jesus Christ is, there is the Catholic Church.*" However, there is not a clear document or date for when the word "orthodox" was used in the context of Christianity. The original Christian Church was simply known as such. It has been suggested that the concept of "Orthodoxy" was used, as early as the second century, to describe those Christians who faithfully adhered to the words of Jesus Christ and the doctrines conveyed by the apostles. For example, in *Adversus Haereses*, written around 180 by the early Christian theologian Irenaeus of Lyons, he refutes the heresies of his time, which he saw as deviating from the true Christian faith, and thus unorthodox. I believe it is logical to conclude that the early Christian Church was catholic by character and orthodox in its teachings.

The Great Schism split the Christian Church into the Catholic Church, the majority of its members in the West, and the Orthodox Church, the majority of its members in the East. While the Western Church kept the title "catholic" and the Eastern Church kept the title "orthodox," both churches describe themselves through the statement of Christian faith, the Nicene Creed, as "*one, holy, catholic and apostolic,*" reflecting a continuity with the original universal church. The Catholic Church represents twenty-three individual churches, including twenty-two Eastern Catholic Rites, one of which is the Maronite Church, and one Western Rite—the Roman Catholic Church, the largest. The Orthodox Church represents seventeen autocephalous churches, with each functioning as an independent and self-governing ecclesiastical body.

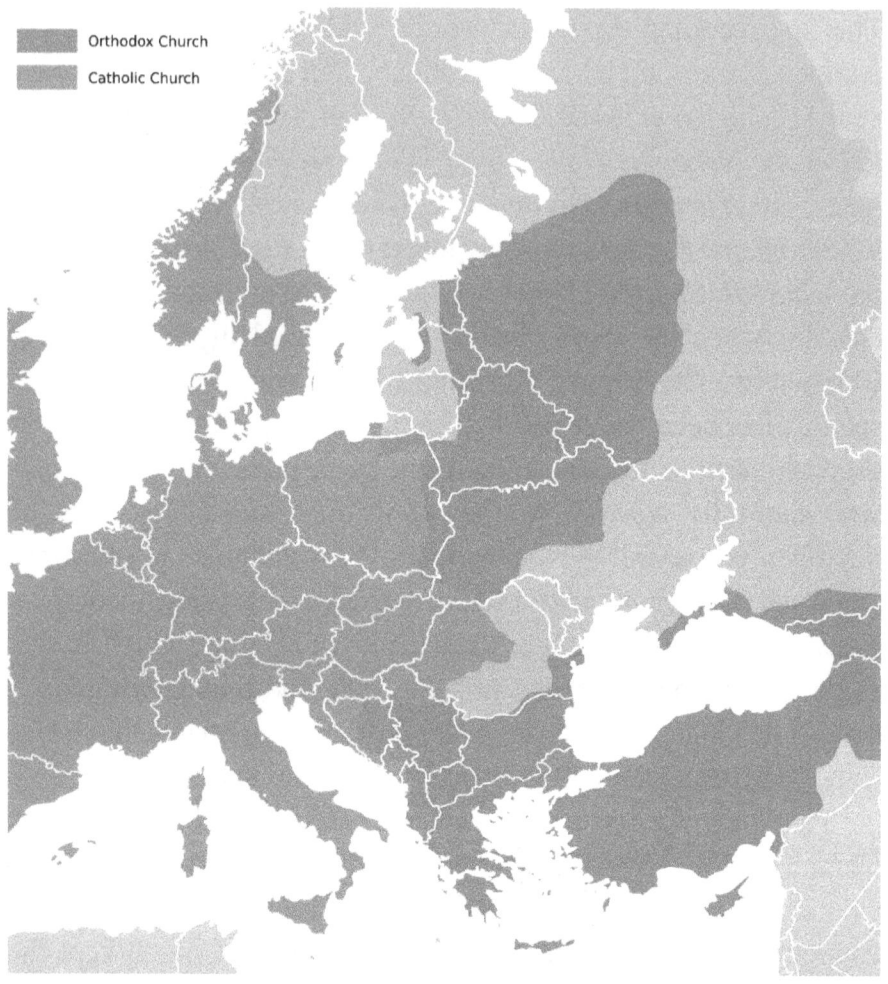

The 1054 East-West Schism

It is important to note that the Maronite Church, even though it is an Eastern Rite, has no counterpart in Orthodoxy. Unlike other denominations, it has remained a unified church within the Eastern tradition from its inception to the present. However, the Maronites did not initially have full communion with Rome until they received recognition from the Pope in 1131, during the Crusades, which was followed by a formal affirmation of their unity with the Roman Catholic Church in 1182.

A Breaking Point

Various factors contributed to the historic division within the two most powerful centers of influence in Christianity at the time. Culture, politics, society, and, most passionately, theology were key contributors, in addition to the most obvious culprits of geography and language. Compounding this was the incompatibility of various civic and religious personalities involved, which collided and came together, along with these other factors, to yield the Great Schism of 1054.

In 1048, a German bishop born as an aristocrat named Bruno of Eguisheim-Dagsburg, in Upper Alsace, present-day France, became Pope Leo IX. He was a reformer and quickly embarked on a mission to strengthen the role of the Pope as the apostolic successor to Saint Peter and affirm his primacy and jurisdiction over all Christians, East and West. With such an important agenda, and given the significance of Constantinople, Pope Leo IX sent three legates to the city in 1054 to meet with Patriarch Michael I Cerularius on his behalf.

This was ostensibly to negotiate an alliance between the Roman and the Byzantine empires in defense against the Normans of Southern Italy, that had become a threat to both Rome and Constantinople, but also to resolve some continuing matters of disagreement between the two sides, including the *Filioque* clause and the authority of the Pope over the Eastern churches.

The group included Humbert of Moyenmoutier, named Archbishop of Sicily in 1050 and renamed Cardinal-Bishop of Silva Candida because he was unable to assume his Sicily post due to objections from the Norman rulers of the island; Frederick of Lorraine, an Archdeacon, a cousin and a prime advisor to Pope Leo

IX, who later became Pope Stephen IX; and Peter, the Archbishop of Amalfi. Despite being warmly welcomed by Byzantine Emperor Constantine IX, who also gave his support for these efforts, months had passed, and Patriarch Cerularius still refused to grant the legates a meeting. Pope Leo IX died in the midst of this standoff without knowing the outcome of his legates' mission and, more importantly, that his emissaries would in the end usher in a schism between Rome and Constantinople, and the rest of the East for that matter, that would last into the present day.

On July 16, 1054, despite the death of Pope Leo IX, Cardinal Humbert of Silva Candida went ahead with his plans and walked into the Holy Wisdom Church, Hagia Sophia, as his legate, and placed a Bull of Excommunication on its main altar to be received as the afternoon prayers began. Patriarch Cerularius, named Patriarch of Constantinople in 1043 by Emperor Constantine IX three years after he became a monk, was the subject of this excommunication, along with his entire clergy. Patriarch Cerularius, in turn, convened a Holy Synod and excommunicated the visiting legates. Countering the assertions of Pope Leo IX, he also took the opportunity to reject the supremacy claim of the Pope as well as Rome's primacy over all Christendom, in essence proclaiming the Byzantine Church's equality with the Roman Church as well as the Church's superiority to the Empire. As would be expected, given the circumstances, the Emperor supported his strong-willed Patriarch.

Originally trained in politics and not religion, Patriarch Cerularius always had the autonomy of the Eastern Church utmost in his mind. His contempt for Rome was equally shared by his lieutenants. The fact that the Byzantine Empire, with Constantinople as its capital, was a direct descendent of the Roman Empire was of no consequence as far as he was concerned. Actually, one reason that led to Patriarch Cerularius' refusal to meet with the papal legates was his knowledge that, in addition to their desire to forge an alliance with him, they had intended to confront him with a letter written by Byzantine Archbishop Leo of Ochrid, criticizing the Western Rite's practice of Christianity. Eventually, however, Patriarch Cerularius' assertion of the Church's superiority over the Empire did not go well with Byzantine Emperor Isaac I, Constantine's successor, who removed the Patriarch from his seat in 1058 shortly before his death in 1059.

Pope Leo IX hailed from a noble dynasty and, as such, he too was skilled in politics, serving both as a religious authority and a secular leader in Italy. In his grievance with the Patriarch of Constantinople, the Pope used whatever means deemed appropriate to deliver his message. The citing of the *"Donation of Constantine,"* which was subsequently determined to be a forgery, was such an example. The Donation of Constantine is a Roman decree attributed to Emperor Constantine I, the first Roman emperor to convert to Christianity. It gave Pope Sylvester I and successive popes dominion over Rome and the remaining parts of the Western Roman Empire as well as Judea, Greece, Asia, Thrace, and Africa. It further stipulated that Constantine retain authority over the Byzantine Empire and its capital of Constantinople.

Neither the high-level delegation of Pope Leo IX nor his invocation of the Donation of Constantine made any positive impression on Patriarch Cerularius. However, the relations between the Christians of the Greek-dominated Byzantine Empire and the Christians of the Latin-dominated Western Roman Empire were now well on their way toward a stalemate, which had been coming about gradually and firmly since the fifth century.

The Schisms of the Early Church

The East–West Schism of 1054 resulted in two state churches, one Greek and one Latin. They are now formally known as the Eastern Orthodox Church and the Roman Catholic Church. Although 1054 represents the definitive break in the Church, several other prior schisms, specifically in the East, had actually taken place during the first millennia of the Church. However, most schisms during that time between Constantinople and Rome healed with the passing of time, but also all managed to contribute to a weakening of Christian unity. Two early schisms are worth noting and discerning, one taking place following the First Ephesian Council in 431 and another, more significant, resulting from the Council of Chalcedon in 451.

The First Ephesian Council, held in 431, was convened by the Roman Emperor Theodosius II (402-450) in Asia Minor in order to resolve disputes stemming from the teachings of Patriarch Nestorius of Constantinople, who asserted the disunity between the natures of Christ as human and Christ as divine. Such teachings were in conflict with the views held by other Byzantine Empire patriarchs, most vocally Cyril of Alexandria, who believed in one nature fully divine and genuinely human. As a result, Patriarch Nestorius was dethroned by the Council and his teachings were determined to be heresy. Nestorius asserted his orthodoxy, and with support particularly from parts of Persia and Asia Minor, a schism ensued resulting in what was called Nestorianism and giving rise to today's Assyrian and Chaldean churches, though with a softened interpretation of Nestorius's original teachings. This ongoing dispute with the Eastern churches regarding the nature of Christ—with the Nestorians arguing for two distinct natures, one divine and one human, existing side-by-side but not united in one person—would not be resolved until twenty years later, and even then, not to the satisfaction of either side.

The Council of Chalcedon was convened by the Emperor Marcian in Bithynia, also in Asia Minor, again to resolve these doctrinal controversies among Eastern theologians over the person and nature of Christ. It too rejected the teachings of another Church leader, this time Patriarch Dioscorus of Alexandria, who was also deposed. Negating the notion of a single nature in Christ, the Council issued a definition affirming hypostasis: the individual person of Jesus Christ possesses two distinct natures, one human and one divine, united in one person without confusion or separation.

Two patriarchs were installed to replace Patriarch Dioscorus, one by the Emperor at the request of the Council and another one appointed locally after the death of Patriarch Dioscorus. This resulted in a split for the Alexandrian Church, giving first rise to the term Melkites, a group loyal to Constantinople, and the Copts, who held onto their views, each with its own Patriarch and theological distinction. Except for this community who continued to teach the one nature of Christ encompassing both Godhead and human personification, the rest of Christendom embraced the definition of Chalcedon on the person and nature of Christ, nonetheless representing a significant theological conflict in the Church of the Byzantine Empire. The nature of Christ remained a subject that continued to cause divisions and disagreements in the Christian Church for many more centuries beyond the Council of Chalcedon.

Another important declaration of the Council of Chalcedon, which also signaled what was to come between the Western and Eastern parts of the Church, was the declaration that while Constantinople, the Empire's center of political and military might, was second in eminence and power, it was, nonetheless, comparable in stature to Rome, the Empire's center of law, order, and civilization. Neither side was satisfied with this declaration. Rome rejected being comparable in stature to Constantinople, and Constantinople was not content with being regarded as second in eminence and power to Rome. Of course, many more complications continued to arise, both in the East as well the West, which further widened the rift. Such difficulties became more frequent and more severe in the ninth century. In addition to the obvious geographic and linguistic divide, faults had already been forming steadily and deeply along the Christian Church's cultural, political, social, and, most severely, theological lines, all combining in a perfect storm that ultimately produced what has now become the Great Schism of 1054.

All schisms in the Christian Church—in both the East and the West, and across large and small denominations—have their own contexts, of which the theological is only one dimension. Understanding the contexts for these schisms provides insight into how they have shaped the Church and influenced modern Christianity. Early schisms, which were primarily centered in the East, focused more on theological differences than on cultural ones. However, given how these differences have blurred over time, it becomes reasonable to consider the role of politics and personalities as well—specifically, how the ambitions of certain individuals or factions may have deepened or solidified divisions. For example, the rivalry between Nestorius of Constantinople and Cyril of Alexandria was a matter of fact, with each working to assert their personal and ecclesiastical influence over the Church, in addition to doctrinal control.

The Great Schism of 1054 marked a definitive division between the Eastern and Western branches of the Church. While theological differences were evident, Pope Leo IX was determined to expand his control and influence, just as Patriarch Michael Cerularius was equally resolute in asserting his exclusive dominance over the Eastern Church. The hardest points to reconcile were less about theology and more about personality and style. I believe personal pride of these two Church leaders made compromise impossible, causing the situation to spiral into a complete break between the East and West. These divisions continued to evolve, especially with the Reformation movement of the 16th century in the Western Church and subsequent division.

CHAPTER 8.

The Provoking Factors of the Schisms

THE FAITH BOND THAT BROUGHT together Christians from both the Eastern and Western empires was strong, but their eventual parting in 1054, although appearing impulsive, was actually the result of a gradual drifting apart that had been building up, and perhaps destined, almost from the onset of the Roman expansion in the East. This expansion began long before the Empire officially embraced Christianity, during a time when very little seemed likely to bring together such diverse civilizations with unique cultural and societal characteristics.

Beginning in the second century, the Roman Empire gradually expanded into Greece, Asia Minor, and the Levant, effectively melding East and West. While the geographic barrier was apparent, it was the least significant obstacle. With the Empire becoming Christian, the East-West interactions increased out of necessity, penetrating all levels of society. Yet, their divergence also grew more pronounced. The two sides lived in different geographies and spoke different languages. Cultural, political, and social factors in their societies were also evolving in opposite directions—stability on one side and disintegration on the other. Most importantly, they practiced divergent traditions in their liturgies, maintained dissimilar religious hierarchies, and quarreled over theological tenets that were a matter of faith.

Geographic Factors

Rome, Constantinople, Alexandria, Antioch, and Jerusalem were the five pillars of the Church at the time, and each was headed by its own Patriarch. The Patriarch in Rome, also doubling as the Pope, was the acknowledged head of all five regional churches. While Jerusalem had its special status because of its significance in early Christianity, Rome, as the papal seat, quickly became the primary Church. When Jerusalem, Alexandria, and Antioch fell to the Arab conquerors, Constantinople, despite two major attacks, remained safe and strong. Still enjoying its special status as the capital of the Byzantine Empire, it became a source of material and moral support to the other three beleaguered Eastern churches, instead of Rome, for sheer kinship and proximity. In many ways, the setting up of an East-West rivalry was becoming obvious to both centers of power.

Linguistic Factors

While not the only spoken language in the East, Greek was certainly a dominant one, perfected by all Christian religious figures, scholars, and other learned people, typically along with Syriac and Hebrew, or whatever native language was spoken by an individual of a certain society. In contrast, the dominate language of the West was entirely Latin. It was unusual at the time for people to acquire fluency in both languages, even for renowned scholars. Thus, for these two communities, the language factor surely added a degree of separation and possibly even confusion when they interacted, even at a leadership level.

Cultural Factors

The hierarchy of the Christian Church, both intentionally and unintentionally, promoted a distinction between the Patriarch of Rome, the religious leader of the entire Western flock, and the patriarchs of the Eastern churches and their parishioners. The Pope, in addition to his role as the Patriarch of the Church of Rome in the West, was also the supreme pontiff for the whole Church. To one side of his Church, the Latin, he was their visible spiritual figure, but to the other side, the Greek, he was a mythical figure with whom they never interacted. This resulted in a duality of loyalty for Christians, in the West to a Pope and in the East to a Patriarch. The patriarchs of the East clearly did not mind this reality, which in fact suited the Patriarch of Constantinople, whose Church was eager to fill such a void.

Political Factors

Despite the geographic, linguistic, and cultural divides between the two communities, successive popes insisted on their universal jurisdiction. The primacy of Rome in the Church was non-negotiable and it stems from Peter and his primacy among the Apostles as well as Peter's own identification with the Church of Rome. The growing influence of the Patriarch of Constantinople over the other three patriarchs of the Byzantine Empire, compounded by the fact that the Emperor, a neighbor of sorts, was a logical supporter of his, was becoming a concern for Rome. The Patriarch of Constantinople's ability to rally other Eastern patriarchs, by then in distress under the Muslim conquest, and unite them against the West was evident. Despite its stature, Constantinople alone against the West would matter little, but with the rest of the Eastern churches joining in, a different situation was emerging.

Social Factors

By the fifth century, when Christianity had spread throughout the Byzantine Empire and was enjoying peace and prosperity, the Western counterpart of the Empire was struggling to defend itself against barbarians' attacks. This eventually led to the disintegration of their society into small fiefdoms and the collapse of their civic institutions. The Roman Pope struggled to fill the power vacuum left by retreating secular bureaucracies and authorities. In contrast, strong imperial power in Constantinople oversaw the civil society and patriarchs presided over Church affairs, with very close cooperation between the two in matters that involved overlapping Church and State administration.

Theological Factors

Theological disputes, typical among the early Christians of the East, eventually troubled the Eastern-Western relations. For centuries, Rome and Constantinople had conflicts on many fronts to contend with. For the most part, minor controversies were resolved by ensuring that the Eastern churches were deferential to Rome, but even the more serious schisms of the first millennium were relatively short and always followed by reconciliation.

One example of such controversies, Quartodecimanism, goes back to the early days of Christianity, when some Eastern communities disagreed with Rome over when to celebrate Easter. They insisted that it should coincide with the full moon, regardless of the day of the week it fell on, just like the Jewish Passover. The Western community wanted to celebrate Easter the following Sunday. Rome eventually prevailed in this matter. Another controversy was brought on by the gradual imposition of clerical celibacy in the West starting in the eighth century. Ordination of married men was the norm throughout the Church, but the ordination of celibate, unmarried men was becoming a requirement for priesthood in the Western Church as early as the fourth century, and for those already married prior to ordination, a total continence in regard to sexual activity also became a requirement. While a ban remained in effect in the West, the Byzantine Empire resolved the matter by rejecting celibacy at the Council of Trullo held in 691. Despite Rome's protest and refusal to accept the outcome of the

Council of Trullo, eventually the difference in approach was acknowledged and accepted. Subsequently, in the ninth century, parts of this resolution from the Council of Trullo were reversed by the Byzantine emperor Leo VI (886-912) to add some restrictions on the marriage of clergy in the East without instituting a total ban.

Unfortunately, not all disputes were always easy to resolve. The use of leavened or unleavened bread in the Eucharist became another major dispute with significant ramifications for the Christian Church. For the Western Church, the bread had to be unleavened, as was the case with the bread served by Jesus to his disciples at the Last Supper. For the Eastern Church, the bread had to be leavened, signifying the Risen Christ. The use of unleavened bread in the Eucharist was one of the reasons that prompted Patriarch Michael Cerularius to attack the West for its Judaic practices, which is said to be a topic that Cardinal Humbert of Silva Candida wanted to discuss on his visit to Constantinople in 1054. But the most serious conflict between East and West occurred when the *"Filioque"* was inserted into the Nicene Creed by the Pope in 1014. The original Greek text of the Nicene Creed was written at the Council of Nicaea in 325 and later expanded at the First Council of Constantinople in 381 to include the part of the Holy Spirit proceeding from the Father; no mention of the Son was made then. The Eastern Churches protested the unilateral change made by the Church of Rome outside the jurisdiction of an ecumenical council.

In the meanwhile, one event that perhaps does not fit any of the categories discussed above but is responsible for accelerating the East-West estrangement is the naming of Charlemagne, the King of the Franks, as Holy Roman Emperor of all Christians by Pope Leo III on Christmas Day 800. Essentially, even though Christian, Charlemagne was viewed as a barbarian king of the Franks, ruling what some felt a polytheist nation. Still, he was installed by the Bishop of Rome to rule over Christendom, which has had a Christian Roman emperor since the inception of Constantinople.

That was a sin that neither the Eastern patriarchs, who were not even consulted on the move, nor their Emperor, who had just been demoted by this move, would be ready to absolve.

Persistent Divisions

The first few centuries immediately following the schism saw events that further aggravated the situation, including the fall of Constantinople in 1204 to the Crusaders and the crowning of a westerner as its Emperor, Baldwin I, albeit for less than one year, as well as the appointment of Western patriarchs to administer the Eastern churches. Soon after, the Western Church itself contended with its tribulations, leading to another major schism, the Protestant Reformation of 1517. Although the impact of the Reformation was of less significance in the East, in general, and in Lebanon specifically, it is relevant to note it as it led to some reform, or perhaps realignment, on the part of some Eastern Christian groups, which will be addressed later in the book.

A 16th-century religious movement by reformers led to another schism, this time within the Roman Catholic Church. It began in 1517 with a criticism of a Catholic Church practice, the sale of indulgences, but quickly evolved into a serious challenge of the Church's doctrines and practices. This movement, according to its leaders, aimed to return to the true teachings of the Bible. However, it led to the creation of a new Christian denomination, appropriately named the Protestant, separate from Rome's authority and Catholic traditions. This Catholic-Protestant schism had immediate and lasting religious, political, and cultural effects in the Western Church and European society. It also prompted Rome to reengage with the Eastern Church.

The original causes of the Great Schism of 1054 can be traced to longstanding doctrinal disputes that developed shortly after Christianity became a formally organized religion, including disagreements over the *Filioque* clause, papal primacy, and liturgical practices. While these theological issues were genuine, they were compounded by deep cultural, linguistic, and political tensions between the Latin West and the Greek East. Moreover, personal ambitions and ecclesiastical rivalries certainly exacerbated the rift, making reconciliation difficult.

However, I believe that the schisms starting in the early Christian Church, especially those that occurred in the East, also represent moments of human failure driven by factors such as misplaced pride, political interference, and theological intransigence. The Great Schism of 1054 exemplifies a division rooted less in irreconcilable doctrine than in cultural difference, historical grievances, and wounded pride. Furthermore, the Western Schism of the 16th century, which occurred within a closer geography and less culturally diverse communities, was certainly about doctrine but fundamentally stemmed from personal and institutional failures.

CHAPTER 9.

The New Denominations of Christianity

IN ADDITION TO THE LITURGICAL, theological, and political changes caused by the schisms, from the time before the Council of Chalcedon in 451 through the Reformation in 1517, a host of new nomenclatures arose. The original Christian Church, and its five founding patriarchates, evolved from a unified entity into churches with fragmented denominations based on theological interpretations of Christ and the structure of ecclesiastical authority. Initially, that was primarily the case in the East. In the West, from 1054 to 1517, the Roman Catholic Church was essentially the dominant Christian tradition. That changed after 1517 with the emergence of Protestant Christians.

The situation in the East, and particularly in the Levant and Lebanon, was more complex. New denominations emerged starting even before the Chalcedonian split and continued after the Great Schism. Another difference in the East was the subsequent reunifications that took place, which did not happen in the West. The various denominations of the Eastern Church, and specifically in Lebanon and the Levant, resulting from the schisms of the early centuries through the East-West schism, are considered next, ordered by their relative size in Lebanon. For completeness and organizational coherence, this discussion also includes the subsequent schisms and reunifications with Rome that primarily occurred during the Ottoman period.

The Antiochene Syriac Maronite Church

The Antiochene Syriac Maronite Church originated in Antioch as a community centered around the followers of Saint Maron, a fourth-century monk whose ascetic community became a distinct ecclesiastical body after his death. Saint Maron's teachings found early acceptance initially in Antioch, where he lived and worshiped, and soon after in Mount Lebanon and other parts of Syria at the hands of his disciples. Aligned with Chalcedonian theology from the beginning, the Maronites eventually expanded widely and deeply into Mount Lebanon, where they developed in relative isolation during the Islamic conquests, allowing them to preserve their autonomy and identity in the remote and safe mountainous regions. By the 12th century, they entered into full communion with the Roman Catholic Church. The Maronite Church follows the West Syriac liturgical tradition, an ancient, Aramaic-centered style of Christian worship that originated in Antioch. Known for its meditative chants, it is unique among Eastern churches for having never broken communion with Rome and for incorporating some aspects of Latin influences in its liturgy.

The Greek Orthodox Church of Antioch

The Antiochene Greek Orthodox are early Christians. They are also known as *Rūm* Orthodox (*Rūm* is an Arabic word that refers to Greek or Byzantine). Their church is Chalcedonian. Some Greek Orthodox originated in Lebanon, particularly in coastal cities, while others sought Lebanon as a refuge. Naturally, the liturgical language is Greek, but Arabic is also used in their religious practices. As with other early Christian communities in Lebanon and the Levant, they trace their roots to the Patriarchate of Antioch.

They were established in 518 subsequent to the disputes resulting from the Council of Chalcedon of 451 and the formation of the Syriac Orthodox Church at that time. As an Eastern Antiochene Church, they were closely affiliated with the Orthodox Church of Constantinople at the time of the Great schism of 1054, functioning as a self-governing church, with the Patriarchate of Constantinople being the highest spiritual authority. As such, they constitute the largest denomination in Eastern Christianity. Their formal presence in Lebanon goes back to the Roman Empire, when Lebanon's coastal cities were dominated by the Greek language and culture, with a noticeable and growing presence of the Aramaic language. Subsequently, as the Eastern side of the Roman Empire evolved into the Byzantine Empire, these cities were becoming important centers of Christianity, and the Greek influence was growing even stronger, giving rise to a visible presence of Orthodox Christianity on the coast as well as in the mountains. Their strong relationship with Byzantine Christianity and theological doctrine as well as their commitment to building religious, educational, and social institutions enabled the Greek Orthodox to create strong foundations for their subsequent growth and longevity in Lebanon and the Levant.

The Greek Orthodox Patriarchate of Antioch split in 1724, when a segment of it established communion with Rome, becoming the Melkite Greek Catholic Church.

The Greek Catholic Church of Antioch

The Antiochene Greek Catholics, or Melkites, are also early Christians. The term "Melkite" derives from the word *melek*, meaning "king" in Aramaic, Hebrew, and Arabic. It originally referred to Christians in the Levant who supported the Byzantine emperor's position on Chalcedonian theology. They are known as *Rūm* Catholic as well. Initially belonging to the Patriarchate of Antioch, as Greek Orthodox, they were aligned with the Patriarch of Constantinople by the time of the 1054 schism. Given their common heritage with Greek Orthodox, some also originated in Lebanon while others sought it as a refuge. Greek is their liturgical language, but Arabic is used in their religious practices as well. Although the Greek Catholics considered reunification with Rome sometime after the schism, this did not materialize until 1724. Their transitioning from their roots as an Eastern Orthodox Church into a new distinct Eastern Catholic Rite in communion with Rome resulted in the creation of the Melkite Greek Catholic Church, governed by the Greek Catholic Patriarch of Antioch, Alexandria, Jerusalem, and all the East. The Melkites, while continuing to adhere to their Byzantine roots, Greek-Antiochene theology, and liturgical language, preserved their Eastern Christian identity as they set out to organize themselves into a visible community with religious, cultural, educational, and social organizations serving their community and establishing their identity in Lebanon and the Levant.

The Melkites were governed by the same Patriarch as the Orthodox, starting in 518, until their unification with Rome in 1724, retaining their ancient Antiochene theological and cultural heritage under their own hierarchy and governance.

The Syriac Orthodox Church of Antioch

Formed in 518, the Syriac Orthodox Church, also referred to as the Jacobite Church, emerged as the main non-Chalcedonian branch from the original Church of Antioch that split off after the disagreements over the Council of Chalcedon ruling in 451. The Syriac Orthodox Church, with a rich liturgical and theological heritage in the Syriac language, belongs to a group referred to as the Oriental Orthodox Christians, who share theological and historical ties with the Coptic and Armenian Orthodox Churches. Its formal name is the Syriac Orthodox Patriarchate of Antioch and All the East. The Syriac Orthodox Church adheres to the West Syriac tradition, developed in Antioch, shaping its theological, liturgical, spiritual, and worship identity. Furthermore, it competes with other Antiochene churches for being the apostolic successor of Saint Peter.

The Syriac Orthodox Patriarchate of Antioch split again in 1662, when the Syriac Catholic Church was formed and established communion with Rome.

The Syriac Catholic Church of Antioch

The Syriac Catholic Church established its union with the Roman Catholic Church gradually and over several centuries, starting in the 17th century. In 1662, a new Patriarch of the Antiochene Syriac Orthodox Church who supported union with Rome was elected. This election and the Patriarch's pro-union stance were immediately opposed by the wider Syriac Orthodox adherents and clergy, leading to interventions that resulted in parallel patriarchal lines. Also, political interference on the part of the Ottoman Caliphate prevented the establishment of an independent and functional Syriac Catholic church. However, in 1783, under a new Patriarch, the church formally concluded its full communion with Rome while preserving its ancient West Syriac liturgical and spiritual traditions.

The Assyrian Church of the East

The Assyrian Church of the East, historically known as the Nestorian Church, although influenced by Antiochene theology, developed outside the Roman Empire, specifically within the Persian Empire. It rejected the decisions of the Council of Chalcedon. Despite this rejection, the Assyrian Church of the East is not considered "Orthodox" in the formal sense of belonging to either the Eastern Orthodox Church or the Oriental Orthodox Church. The reason why it does not belong to these non-Chalcedonian churches is because the Assyrian Church of the East did not participate in the Council of Chalcedon, as it was located outside the Roman imperial territory. The Assyrian Church of the East is credited with spreading Christianity in parts of Persia, Central Asia, India, and China. The East Syriac tradition, distinct from the West Syriac tradition, developed further east in the Persian Empire and formed the historical theological and liturgical identity of the Assyrian Church of the East.

The Assyrian Church of the East split in 1552, when the Chaldean Catholic Church was formed and established communion with Rome.

The Chaldean Catholic Church

The Chaldean Catholic Church was established in 1552, when a schism within the Assyrian Church of the East led a faction to enter into union with Rome while preserving the East Syriac theology and liturgy. Its formal recognition by Rome included full acceptance of Chalcedon's Christological teachings but also allowing them to maintain their own hierarchy. Now based in Baghdad, the Chaldean Catholic Church reflects both Persian and Syriac Christian traditions. Its spiritual roots remain in the same East Syriac tradition as the Assyrian Church of the East, preserving an ancient identity with a liturgy influenced by Antiochene theology, even though it is not formally tied to Antioch.

The Armenian Apostolic Church

As one of the oldest churches, the Armenian Apostolic Church was formed in 301, when Armenia became the first nation to adopt Christianity as a state religion, with its own language, liturgy, and theological identity. It formally rejected the rulings of the Council of Chalcedon in 506, and became part of Oriental Orthodoxy, alongside the Syriac and Coptic Churches. Located geographically in the East and sharing cultural and theological roots with the Greek and Syriac churches, the Armenian Apostolic Church was not part of the Church of Antioch and had actually severed ties with both Rome and Constantinople in 610.

The Armenian Apostolic Church split in 1742, when the Armenian Catholic Church was formed and established communion with Rome.

The Armenian Catholic Church

The Armenian Catholic Church was formed in 1742, when a subset of the Armenian Apostolic Church accepted the Christological teachings of the Council of Chalcedon and entered into full communion with the Roman Catholic Church, under Pope Benedict XIV. Retaining their unique Armenian liturgical traditions and identity, this union prevailed after a number of prior attempts, including during the Crusades and subsequent Caliphates. Based in Lebanon, highlighting its prominent roots in the Levant, the Armenian Catholic Church is not part of the Church of Antioch but shares its Eastern Christian heritage.

The Coptic Orthodox Church of Alexandria

Formed in 42, the Coptic Church is also part of Eastern Orthodoxy, belonging to the ancient Church of Alexandria. The Coptic Church is non-Chalcedonian in communion with the Oriental Orthodox Christian churches. In fact, the Coptic Orthodox Church was at the center of the theological dispute with the Council of Chalcedon's ruling in 451. The Patriarch of the Church of Alexandria also holds the title of Pope. The Coptic Orthodox Church maintains its own liturgical Coptic language, liturgy, and distinctive monastic traditions.

The Coptic Orthodox Church of Alexandria split in 1895, when the Coptic Catholic Church was formed and established communion with Rome.

The Coptic Catholic Church

The Coptic Catholic Church arose in the 18th century, when a small segment of the Coptic Orthodox Church sought union with Rome. It traces its heritage back to the Coptic Orthodox Church of Alexandria and retains its distinct Coptic theological and liturgical tradition. In 1895, Pope Leo XIII formally established the Coptic Patriarchate of Alexandria, with its patriarchal seat in Cairo, thus entering into full communion with the Roman Catholic Church. The Coptic Catholic Church maintains its own organizational structure while preserving its own ancient Coptic rituals.

Rapprochement and Reconciliation

Since the schism of 1054, many of the fundamental East-West differences, particularly theological ones, have remained. Concessions and attempts at rapprochement were made, especially in the early periods, achieving some limited success toward reconciliation; however, full reunion remained elusive. Although at a slow pace, relations between the Catholic and Orthodox churches have improved. It is relevant to note that while ultimately all other Eastern churches joined the Patriarch of Constantinople in his 1054 schism with Rome, one group, the Maronites, did not. However, as a result of their retreat deep into Mount Lebanon, starting in the seventh century, in search of a safe haven away from advancing Muslim forces, the Maronites were left in almost total isolation from the outside world, including Rome. It was not until the 11th century that the Crusaders, on their way to Jerusalem, reconnected with the Maronites in Mount Lebanon. The Crusaders and the Christians in Lebanon developed a strong bond, especially with the Maronites. This relationship eventually led to the formal establishment of the Maronite full communion with Rome in 1182, which has persisted despite the subsequent isolation as a result of the Caliphates' return after the end of the Crusades.

The New Denominations of Christianity

Although much later, in the 16th century, the Rome-Maronite communion paved the way for a number of other groups in the Eastern Rite Catholic Churches, which had earlier supported the Patriarch of Constantinople, to follow suit. As part of the reconciliation agreement and their consenting to the primacy of Rome, they have retained their Eastern liturgical and theological traditions, as well as administrative structures, including their patriarchs.

The Byzantine Empire was ethnically and culturally diverse, encompassing Phoenicians, Jews, Greeks, Syriacs, Armenians, Copts, Persians, Arabs, Berbers, and more. Disagreements, naturally, were often difficult to reconcile. What might have begun as a purely theological disagreement could quickly degenerate into personal or communal discord—and the opposite is true. It is clear to me that the resulting churches and denominations mirror this Eastern society and its diversity. However, viewed through a modern lens, many of these doctrinal differences appear less monumental than they once seemed, especially as the positions of both Catholic and Orthodox Churches have evolved, and mutual understanding has grown.

While doctrinal—or terminological—issues certainly existed, they were often intensified by an inability among groups to accept diversity of belief, sometimes compounded by human shortcomings. The divisions that once seemed intractable now often appear more reflective of historical and sociopolitical contexts than of truly irreconcilable theological truths. Important distinctions exist, but arguably they do not warrant the enduring institutional division Christianity has experienced for nearly a millennium.

Moreover, many of the communities that found themselves excluded—whether by their choice or the decision of others—have survived and managed to preserve their ancient traditions, and in some cases have even evolved from their earlier positions. This indicates that authorities may have at times rushed to judgment in seeking or enforcing separations. More likely, they often allowed politics and personalities to resolve theological questions. Despite the damage caused by these divisions, they have also given rise to a rich tapestry of traditions within the Christian faith and, just as importantly, left a legacy of renewed thought, identity, and expression.

CHAPTER 10.

The Crusades

BY THE END OF THE 11th century, the Byzantine Empire had lost considerable portions of its territory to the Seljuks. At the same time, Western Europe was becoming a significant power. The Seljuks' victories against the Byzantine Empire in Asia Minor and the continued occupation of Jerusalem by the Fatimids eventually triggered a response. The Crusades (1095-1291) were launched, in part, as an effort to restore access to Christian holy sites in Jerusalem, which had come under Muslim control. Severe restrictions imposed on pilgrims visiting Jerusalem's holy places galvanized Christians of Western Europe—encouraged by their Eastern counterparts—to launch this series of military campaigns. Nine Crusades, in total, were undertaken over nearly two hundred years, with a stated aim to protect Christian pilgrims and assert religious and political influence in the region.

Jerusalem fell to the Crusaders in 1099, establishing Latin Christian rule over the city after a protracted siege. As they marched toward Jerusalem, they also captured the important Byzantine cities of Nicaea, Iconium, Caesarea Mazaca, and Antioch, which were then occupied by the Seljuks. Subsequently, the Crusaders gained control of the Lebanese coast, starting with Tripoli in 1109, and then Beirut and Sidon in 1110, and finally Tyre in 1124.

In 1095, and despite the fact that relations between Christians in the East and those in the West had been strained, the Roman Emperor Alexius I (1081-1118) asked Pope Urban II for his help in confronting the Turkish threat. Alexius' request was met with immediate acceptance when the Pope called on the Christians under his jurisdiction to aid the Byzantines in launching a military campaign to recapture the Holy Land. This request marked the beginning of what became nearly a two-hundred-year struggle, wars initiated and supported by the Church, in both its Western and Eastern branches. These Holy Land military interventions had as their initial and primary objective securing Jerusalem and its surrounding areas, conquered by the Rashidun Caliphate centuries earlier, and held by succeeding Caliphates, under Christian rule.

Impact on Christians in Lebanon

The arrival of the Crusaders in Lebanon in 1099, on their way to Jerusalem, brought the Christians much needed relief, increased autonomy, and recognition, at least for some time. Holed up in their fortified Lebanese mountain strongholds, and essentially cut off from any significant relations with the outside world throughout the reign of Muslim Caliphates, the Christians in Lebanon re-emerged and quickly re-established relations with Western Christianity. Specifically, the Maronites allied with and assisted the Crusaders as they marched toward Jerusalem, which did not sit well with the Caliphate rulers. However, this helped the Christians enhance their status and provided them some protection.

Lebanon came under the Crusaders' control as a strategic passage for reaching and defending Jerusalem. To that end, they built castles and citadels, including the well-known Tripoli, Byblos, and Sidon citadels. These large structures were used to defend strongholds and guard routes to the Holy Land. Also, these castles served as homes for the ruling class in the new Crusaders' states that were created in the region. They have remained as important landmarks of Lebanon's heritage into the present.

The Maronite Patriarchate, established under Yohanna Mārūn in 685, was in contact, but not in communion, with Rome. However, in 1131, the Maronite Patriarch Gregorious Al Halati received communication from Pope Innocent II of Rome recognizing the Maronite Church as a self-governing Eastern Rite Catholic Church. This affiliation was affirmed in 1182 by Patriarch Peter of Lehfed and his bishops, under Pope Lucius III, and has remained unbroken to this day, although the Maronites hold strongly that their church was always in communion with the Holy See.

In 1199, Jeremiah Al Amchiti was elected as Maronite Patriarch and became the first patriarch to visit Rome at the invitation of Pope Innocent III to attend the Fourth Council of the Lateran in 1215. This visit ushered in a period of closeness between Rome and the Maronites, which led to the Maronites' adoption of Latin practices in their liturgy.

Next, the first four consequential Crusades are briefly discussed. Remaining ones are considered together.

The First Crusade (1096-1099)

From the point of view of the participating Western nations and the Byzantine Empire, the First Crusade was a success. Fighting forces departed Clermont, France, for Constantinople in August 1096. In May 1097, the Crusaders and their Byzantine allies surrounded Nicaea, the Seljuks' capital in Anatolia. The city surrendered in late June. The joint Crusaders and Byzantine forces continued their march through Anatolia, freeing Antioch in June 1098. Next, the Crusaders began their march toward Jerusalem, then occupied by the Fatimids. A besieged Jerusalem surrendered in 1099. To govern the conquered territory, four Crusader states were established: County of Edessa (1098-1150), Principality of Antioch (1098-1268), County of Tripoli (1102-1289), and Kingdom of Jerusalem (1099-1291).

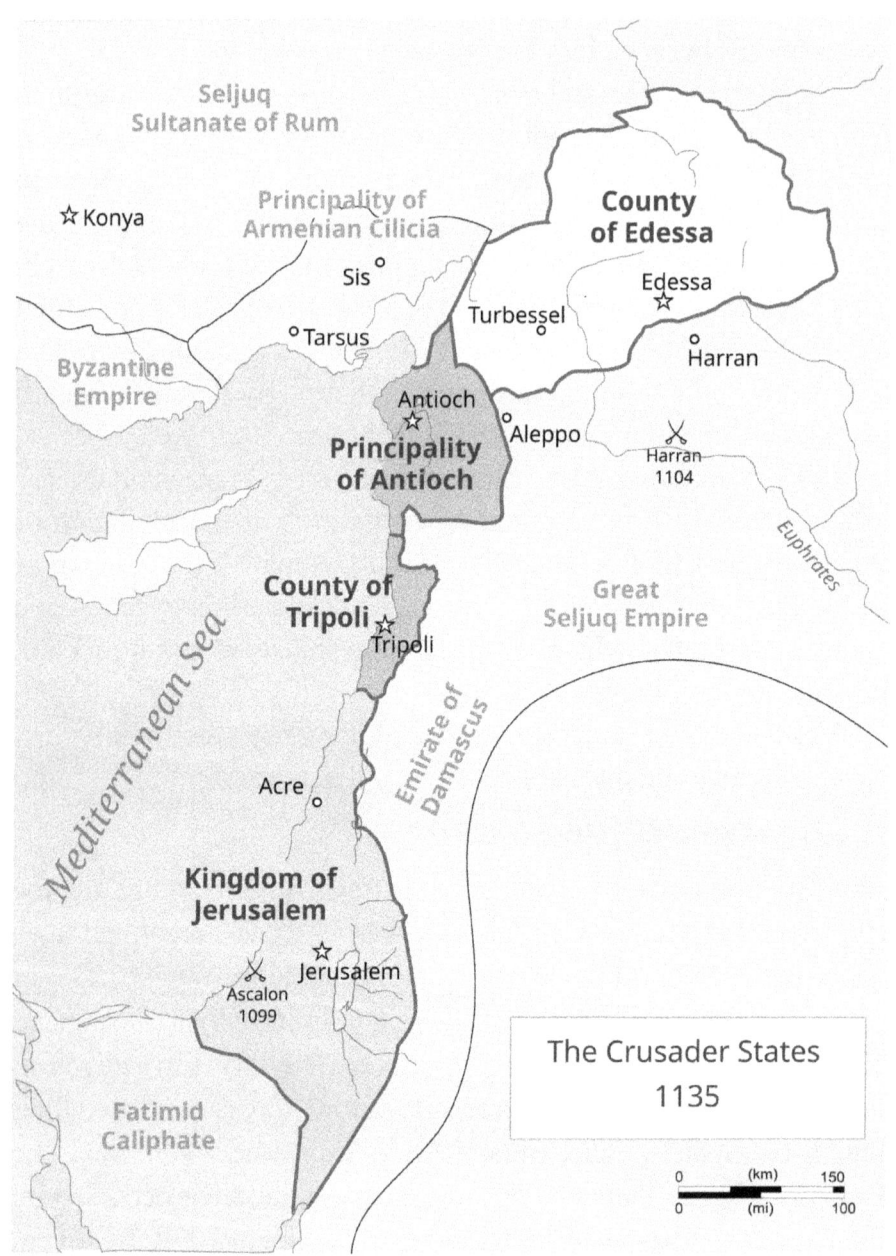

The Crusader States

The Second Crusade (1147-1149)

Retaining control in the region until around 1130, Muslim forces began gaining ground in their own *jihad*, recapturing land from the Crusaders. Thus, the Second Crusade to reclaim Edessa, in Upper Mesopotamia, which was reoccupied by the Seljuks in 1144. An attempt to capture nearby Damascus was also thwarted by the Seljuks. The Crusaders made few advances and suffered heavy losses in both instances as well as in their quest to regain what they had lost in the Holy Land.

The Third Crusade (1187-1192)

The goal of the Third Crusade was to recapture Jerusalem. In 1187, Saladin began a major campaign against the Crusader Kingdom of Jerusalem, taking back the city along with a large amount of territory. In September 1191, Crusader forces defeated those of Saladin and recaptured the cities of Jaffa and Acre, approaching Jerusalem. In 1192, the Crusaders and Saladin signed a peace treaty that re-established the Kingdom of Jerusalem, though without the city of Jerusalem itself, which remained under the Ayyubids' control. However, the city was reopened for Christian pilgrims, providing a reason to end the war.

The Fourth Crusade (1202-1204)

The Fourth Crusade was yet another attempt to free Jerusalem from Muslim rule, but instead it turned into power struggles within and between the West and the Byzantine Empire. The animosity resulting from prior campaigns had reached new heights by now, a full century since the launch of the first Crusade in 1099. Claiming an about face on the part of the Byzantines, even undermining the Crusaders' efforts, this was seen as an act of revenge by the Crusaders who declared war on Constantinople, the capital of the Byzantine Empire. This was a major blow to East-West relations, ending with the devastating Fall of Constantinople in 1204 and establishing the Latin Empire in its place. This act of the Crusaders, which became known as The Sack of Constantinople, resulted in much bloodshed, destruction, and the ruining of ancient art, let alone deepening the distrust and increasing animosity between the Eastern and Western churches.

Although the Sack of Constantinople was a devastating event that severely weakened the Byzantine Empire, and perhaps a key turning point that accelerated the empire's decline, the Latin Empire in Constantinople was short-lived, ending in 1261 when the Byzantine Empire recaptured the city.

The Final Crusades (1208-1291)

Throughout the remainder of the 13th century, a variety of Crusades—the fifth to the ninth—were launched to free the Holy Land. However, these campaigns were undermined by forces that had already suffered significant attrition of troops and damage to equipment during earlier combat, ultimately rendering them ineffective in achieving their operational objectives. These campaigns became barely connected to the original goal, fighting in many locations and with various groups seen as enemies of the Christian faith. The best way to describe these efforts would be that the Crusaders lost their way. This led to significant weakening of the Crusades. One exception worth mentioning is the Sixth Crusade (1228-1229), when the Crusaders were able to free Jerusalem in 1229, holding it until 1244, when it was lost again to the Ayyubid dynasty. Notably, this was not the result of any act of war but through diplomatic negotiations.

In 1291, one of the only remaining Crusader cities, Acre, fell to the Muslim Mamluks, marking the end of the Crusader States and the Crusades themselves. Despite the nine major Crusades, Muslim domination persisted throughout the region.

While it predates the Crusades, the Great Schism of 1054 also caused a structural division within Christianity that was subsequently exacerbated by the Crusades. Although the primary objective of the Crusades was to reclaim the Holy Land, these underlying tensions led to further discord among Christians that also amplified the animosities resulting from the Great Schism.

Migration to Cyprus

The conquests and their harsh ramifications on Christians in Lebanon prompted some to consider a safer refuge in areas still controlled by the Byzantines. With migration at the time limited to easily reached geographic locations that were safe and, logically, westward, the Island of Cyprus seemed appealing. Thus, a small number of Christians, mostly Maronites, began to move to the northern part of Cyprus during the eighth and ninth centuries. However, the majority of the Christians who moved to Cyprus, particularly the Maronites, did not leave on their own accord. Often, this was the result of mutual self-serving alliances and arrangements between Caliphate rulers and Byzantine rulers in order to weaken the Christian resistance in Mount Lebanon and ease the attacks by the Marada and Maronites on their harsh occupiers.

Another wave of migration to Cyprus began subsequently. In 1192, as the Crusaders and Saladin were fighting over Jerusalem and, naturally, Lebanon was feeling some of the resulting consequences, another group of Christians, also mostly Maronites, headed to Cyprus, joining retreating Crusaders. The Christians, but the Maronites in particular, were aligned with the Crusaders and enjoyed protection during their reign. Not surprisingly, the defeat of the Crusaders in the Holy Land heightened their anxiety about being subjugated to more Muslim rule again.

The Maronites lived on the island peacefully, attempting to create what they had in Mount Lebanon in order to preserve their faith and culture. Others soon followed, creating a community with a Maronite bishop assigned to it as early as 1340. This wave of Christian migration also extended to Malta and Rhodes.

It is noteworthy that this is considered the first instance of significant numbers of Christians leaving Lebanon in search of a new refuge during this time period. This exodus would not be the last.

Ramifications of the End of the Crusades on the Lebanese Christians

With the defeat of the Crusaders and, more severely, the fall of essentially all remaining remnants of the Byzantine Empire, Muslim forces were again in a position to bring the Levant back under the rule of the Caliphates, which would last until 1918. This consolidation further isolated the Christians of the East, especially in Lebanon, for an extended period of time.

The period of the Crusades marked an important milestone in the history of the Christians in Lebanon. One of the Crusaders' interests in Lebanon was to control important coastal cities that would serve as military and logistics hubs in their quest to free the Holy Land. After their victory in the First Crusade, they quickly set up a number of states in the Levant, including one in Lebanon. Notable is the County of Tripoli (1109-1289), covering significant parts of Lebanon's and Syria's coast. These Crusader states were primarily meant to keep control of freed territories, facilitate additional land acquisition, keep the road to Jerusalem safe, and help defend Christians in the Levant.

After nearly two hundred years of European control, the conflict was coming to an end with the defeat of the Crusaders. The strong relationship between the Crusaders and Lebanese Christians brought subsequent ramifications to the Christians when Muslim rule returned in 1291. The Mamluks, who took control of Lebanon and much of the Levant from the Crusaders, launched a campaign that drove away or killed many Western Christians and then turned onto Eastern Christians for retribution.

Lebanese Christians faced persecution once again, first from the Mamluks, who destroyed churches and massacred Christians, and then from the Ottomans, who aggravated the great famine that killed half of Mount Lebanon's population during the First World War. And, in the end, Muslim domination persisted throughout the region.

Although the Crusaders failed in their original mission, their relations with the Christians of Lebanon, especially the Maronites, were among the most enduring. With France as a major force in the Crusades, that nation maintained interest in the region and its Christian population. This alliance would prove beneficial in subsequent stages of Lebanon's development.

Of significant importance for the future of Lebanon, the strong organizational structures put in place by the Christian leadership during the period of the Crusades enabled their communities to continue to govern their own religious and social affairs, despite the loss of Western protection. Under their patriarchs and bishops—who operated from the monasteries and churches they developed during earlier times—the Church provided spiritual guidance, coordinated community efforts, and represented the people in negotiations with the returning Muslim rulers.

PART THREE

From the Mamluks to the Lebanese Diaspora

CHAPTER 11.

The Return of the Caliphates and Expanding Western Relations

THE SENSE OF SECURITY AND safety felt by the Christians under the Crusaders soon dissipated with the return of the last two Muslim dynasties, first the Mamluks and then the Ottomans. Having expanded their footprints beyond their traditional geography during the reign of the Crusades, many Christians retreated to remote areas and mountainous regions where they once were able to practice their faith freely under the restrictive rules of earlier Caliphates. With the Crusaders gone and the Mamluks taking their place toward the end of the 13th century, Christians maintained the strength of their communities by relying on the sophisticated church and civil organizations they had built. This religious and cultural support allowed the Christians to focus on their basic necessities and thrive in their local communities despite suffering from violence at the hands of the Mamluks and Ottomans. The Christians' organizational skills and abilities, honed and perfected during a long period of vulnerability and occupation, played a critical role in preserving their religious and cultural traditions.

The Mamluks

As the Crusaders stumbled, a new dynasty, the Mamluks (1250-1517), was taking shape in Egypt, reestablishing Sunni rule in most of the territories under the Crusaders' control, including in Lebanon. The Mamluks, who made Cairo their capital, were an ethnically diverse group, but primarily Turkic, from Central Asia. Historically, in this context, the term Mamluk refers to slave soldiers who served, protected, and fought on behalf of the Caliphates going back to the Abbasids. The Mamluks came into being when descendants of originally enslaved mercenaries, who had risen to the ranks of generals and high-ranking soldiers, overthrew the Ayyubids and established their own dynasty by rebelling against, and toppling, the last Ayyubid Sultan in Egypt.

The Mamluks were especially harsh on the Christian population because of their support for the Crusaders and wasted no time taking revenge on them soon after they took full control. This kind of behavior essentially continued, in various intensities, throughout their rule. One such episode was in 1267, when many towns in Mount Lebanon were destroyed, churches and monasteries demolished, captives beheaded, and crops devastated. The Mamluks were able to capture Antioch early, in 1268, but took longer to capture the Canaanite plains. Specifically, cities of the Lebanese coast, starting with Tripoli, began to fall one after the other, from 1289 to 1291, to the advancing Mamluk forces. At this time, they were able to decisively end the Crusaders' presence in the Levant, culminating with Acre's fall in 1291.

As with prior Caliphates, the Mamluks considered the Christians *dhimmis*, granting them some protections but also placing on them many restrictions. They were barred from holding certain positions of power or participating in public religious expression as they were able to do under the Crusaders. The Mamluks were less tolerant of Christians than some earlier Muslim rulers and viewed Christians with suspicion due to their persistent strong relations with the West and former alliances with the Crusaders. They strictly enforced *dhimmi* regulations, imposed heavy taxes leading to significant hardships, often destroyed churches and prevented the building of new ones, and prohibited public Christian practices. Although, in some cases, Christians were pressured to convert to Islam to escape persecution, they resisted. However, geographic isolation of some regions posed economic challenges causing some Christians to convert to Islam in order to avoid a *jizya* burden they could not afford.

The Maronites, building on reestablished relations during the Crusades, were able to maintain strong ties with the Vatican and European states. Their alignment with the Roman Catholic Church during the 12th century created a strong bond that persisted despite the returning walls of isolation. This close relationship was not without cost, though, as it became a point of contention with the Mamluks. In 1367, the Mamluks captured and killed the Maronite Patriarch Gabriel of Hjoula, who was burnt at the stake in the city of Tripoli.

Fleeing persecution during the Mamluk rule as well, more Shia Muslims migrated to the Beqaa and areas in Mount Lebanon from Syria, Iraq, and Arabia. Facing the same fate, Christians, Shia, and Druze often launched protest rebellions in Mount Lebanon against brutal treatment by the Mamluks. In fact, the Mamluks were equally hostile to the Shia and cracked down on their practices, destroyed their religious sites, and targeted their leaders, prompting more waves of Shia migration toward South Lebanon. However, Shia communities in Jabal Amel still faced particularly severe persecution.

As with previous Islamic rulers, the Mamluks maintained the *dhimmi* status for Jews, who were subject to the *jizya*. Although generally pragmatic on this front, the Mamluks presided over periods marked by discrimination and forced conversions against

Jewish communities. Despite these challenges, Jews continued to play an important role in Lebanese society, including involvement in trade and commerce.

The Black Death

As if the cruelty of the Mamluks and accumulated hardships going back to earlier dynasties were not enough, a wave of Black Death, a bubonic plague pandemic, starting in 1347, hit much of the geographic area under Mamluk rule, including Lebanon. Wreaking havoc on many parts of Europe, the pandemic spread swiftly and intensely, impacting many places in the East in addition to Europe and lasting for four years, or more depending on the region. Additional waves followed, covering more of Europe, the Near/Middle East, much of Asia, and all of North Africa.

By numerous estimates, Lebanon, as well as many other nations, lost anywhere from a third to one-half of its total population, causing not only suffering but also severe economic and social disruptions. While the outbreak subsided and the pandemic was declared under control by 1351, it did not disappear entirely. The deadly plague resurfaced periodically over the following centuries, striking in waves across Lebanon and other areas within the territories of the Mamluk dynasty and Ottoman Caliphate, lasting well into the 17th century.

Expanding Western Relations—Latinization and Cultural Renaissance

Despite occupation, this was a period when the Christians were able to look outward and seek influential spiritual and intellectual connections with relations they cultivated during the Crusades. Two such consequential East-West events were the Maronite Synods of 1580 and 1596, held in Mount Lebanon.

The 1580 Synod took place in Qannoubine and involved the Maronite Church leaders and legates of Pope Gregory XIII. The synod was organized to expand on early Latinization efforts going back to the time of the Crusades, including the affirmation, by the Maronites, of decisions taken at the Council of Trent, on theology as well as reforms within the Catholic Church. As a result of the Synod, the Maronites, eager to solidify their communion with Rome, accepted the addition of the *Filioque* ("... *the Father and the Son*") to the Nicene Creed. This was not, in any way, a change in position as the Maronites had already accepted the Council of Chalcedon's decision back in 451. They also introduced sacramental practices of the Roman Catholic Rite into their own practices and began to use Roman chalices and vestments. More significantly, the Maronites accepted new molds for making hosts, given to them by visiting legates. This marked the beginning of their use of unleavened bread in Communion, bringing them in total conformity with the Council of Trent and thus with prevailing Roman Catholic practices.

Another case in point regarding the Maronites' close cooperation with Rome is the formation of the Pontifical Maronite College of Rome, an important outcome of the 1580 Synod. It was founded in 1584 to train Maronite clergy. Students were taught in the Eastern Christian tradition, including Syriac. Their education was instrumental in promoting intellectual growth and introducing Western ideas in Lebanon and other Levantine countries. In turn, they were able to raise awareness in Europe about the challenges faced by Eastern Christianity. Upon their return to Lebanon, graduates of the Maronite College led efforts to reform religious practices in the Levant and continued to strengthen relations with Rome. Many priests who trained in the Maronite College became noted scholars, prominent patriarchs, and bishops, who influenced the intellectual and cultural development of the church and Lebanon. Furthermore, Maronite clergy played an important role in the revival and preservation of the Arabic language and literature as a result of their participation in these intellectual and cultural exchanges, including the translation of important Arabic texts into other languages and, conversely, disseminating Western literature in Arabic.

A noted product of the Pontifical Maronite College of Rome is the Fifty-Seventh Patriarch of the Maronites, Venerable Estephan El Douaihy, born in 1630. He is a famed scholar and recognized historian of the Maronite Church and one of the longest serving patriarchs, having served in this role from 1630, at age forty, until his death in 1670. Estephan El Douaihy started his seminary studies at the Maronite College, at age eleven, and stayed there for fourteen years. Patriarch El Douaihy resisted Ottomans on many fronts, but particularly for their harsh taxation policies that were often unaffordable for many Christian peasants. Because of this, he was always on the move to avoid arrest. Patriarch El Douaihy was beatified in August 2024.

The 1596 Maronite Synod was also held in Qannoubine at the request of Pope Clement VIII, who dispatched another legate on a mission to Lebanon to continue the reforms that began with the 1580 Synod. By then, the first graduates from the Pontifical Maronite College of Rome had come back to Lebanon and were already working on implementing what they had learned in their Roman Catholic training. This Synod called for finalizing ritual congruence and uniformity of practice, such as the use of only unleavened bread in the Divine Liturgy and the use of the 1592 Roman Mass. Although the Synod of 1596 aimed to ensure standardization, the conveners allowed the Maronite Church to determine how and when certain changes, such as the separation of the three sacraments of Baptism, Confirmation, and Holy Eucharist, could be carried out. At the time, the three sacraments were given at once in the Maronite Rite and, in actuality, this is one of the changes that was never implemented as Baptism and Confirmation continue to be done at the same time after the birth of a child.

The Mamluk legacy in Lebanon, as in many parts of the Levant, was both destructive and constructive. Early on, their focus was to completely banish European presence from the region, specifically the Crusaders' influence. The Maronite Church's alignment with the Papacy, established shortly after the Crusaders arrived in Lebanon, nurtured Western relations. Over time, Western engagement, which began with religion during the Crusades, had strengthened and expanded to include trade, culture, and diplomacy—often all intertwined.

The Mamluks understood that it would be difficult to undo these relations, as Western interest in the Holy Land—including Lebanon—persisted despite the physical departure of the Crusaders. Christians increasingly looked to Western Europe for political protection as well as cultural exchange. The Mamluks also realized that they could exploit the coastal ports, built in major Lebanese cities during the Crusades, especially the Port of Beirut, to support their trade initiatives with European states. These relations, which continued to strengthen under both the Mamluks and Ottomans, eventually shaped the pluralistic and liberal Lebanese society that facilitated Lebanon's later role as a bridge between East and West.

CHAPTER 12.

The Ottoman Caliphate and Consequential Occupation in Lebanon

THE OTTOMAN CALIPHATE (1299-1918) PERSISTED for more than six hundred years, the longest lasting Muslim ruler. Although the Ottomans did not claim direct familial descent from the Prophet, as with the earlier Caliphates, their conquest of Mecca and Medina allowed them to claim spiritual authority over the Muslim world.

Perhaps in ways different than any other Caliphate ruling Lebanon before them, the Ottomans caused disruptions in nearly every aspect of Lebanese society, lasting into the present time. This reality, along with the fact that there remains so much oral history from the Ottoman era etched in the psyche of the Lebanese, warrants thorough and careful consideration, more than any prior Caliphate.

Even though they defeated the Mamluks, it was the Seljuks who gave rise to the Ottomans. All three dynasties share the Turkic background. The Seljuk Turks originated in Central Asia, and the Ottoman Turks originated in Northwestern Asia Minor. However, the Ottomans are considered to have come into power through the remnants of the Seljuks, and then subsequently created their own empire. Earlier, the Ottoman Turks had also served as slaves and warriors under the Abbasids and rose to positions of prominence within this dynasty because of their courage and discipline.

Constantinople, the capital of the Byzantine Empire, and a nearby city of the Ottomans' origin, served as the capital for the Ottoman Caliphate, renaming it Istanbul. The Ottoman Caliphate controlled significant parts of Southeastern Europe, Southwestern Asia, and North Africa. During its reign, the Empire was both a destabilizing force in the region and creator of an unintentional bond between the Eastern and Western civilizations.

Unlike Muslim dynasties before them, the Ottomans tolerated other religious beliefs, to a point, not because of good will, but out of necessity and astuteness. A large number of the people falling under their control were primarily Christian whose well-established Church hierarchy and feudal class desired to secure and maintain their religious autonomy and land. This resonated with the Ottomans, but there was no escaping paying the *jizya* and, at times, the more concerning risk of conscription. The Ottomans practiced local rule by creating decentralized administrative structures for their territories and appointed regional leaders, or feudal lords, reporting directly to them, as they oversaw the needs of their people and collected the taxes on behalf of the Empire. To ensure allegiance to the Sultan and to keep their grip on power, they perfected the policies of divide and conquer.

The Ottomans in Lebanon

Despite its 1299 inception, the Ottoman Caliphate did not conquer Lebanon until 1516, under Sultan Selim, dominating it for more than four hundred years through the end of the First World War in 1918. Thus, the impact of the Ottoman Caliphate on Lebanon has been a lasting one. It is fair to say that the Christians in Lebanon suffered at the hands of this Caliphate in similar ways, sometimes more, than they did under earlier ones. However, the

Ottomans were much more interested in collecting the *jizya* than prior rulers and thus more willing to grant the Christians some degree of autonomy in return for any and all forms of monetized assets. Accordingly, some parts of Lebanon enjoyed relative self-rule during the Ottoman period, particularly in Mount Lebanon. To ensure tight control over their Empire's population, and maximize the *jizya* collection, the Ottomans eventually developed an elaborate census to account for and keep track of every person living in the cities and villages within their sphere of influence.

Religious dynamics in Lebanon shifted constantly under the rule of controlling empires. The well-established Byzantine and Maronite Christian strongholds enjoyed, for the most part, relative isolation and independence during periods of foreign rule in their remote mountains. Such enclaves eventually became attractive as a refuge for others also escaping persecution, such as the non-Sunni Muslim minorities living under Sunni rules who migrated to Mount Lebanon in search of their own religious freedom. Among these were the Shia, who had migrated from the Arabian Peninsula and settled in South Lebanon and the Beqaa region. The same was true of the Druze, who had earlier fled persecution in Egypt, as an offshoot of Shia, to their own refuge in Mount Lebanon and parts of South Lebanon. The Druze found a way to ingratiate themselves with the dominant Ottomans, which brought them significant local clout and authority. That was not the case with the Shia. Although the Ottomans followed a policy of marginalization of Shia in Lebanon, they did not implement widespread persecution.

The Ottoman Caliphate governed non-Muslim communities through the millet system. The Turkish word "millet," or *milla* in Arabic, refers to a certain unique religious denomination. Each such community was granted a degree of autonomy in religious and civil matters to oversee their affairs through their own religious systems and institutions. For example, Christians were grouped into different religious millets (e.g., Maronites, Greek Orthodox,

Melkites), each led by their own religious leaders. These leaders were responsible for administering their community's internal affairs, including birth, marriage, death, and education. Feudal lords were responsible for taxation, while ensuring loyalty to the Ottomans. This enabled the Christians, despite living under a Caliphate, to maintain their already formed strong communal organization that had contributed to their ability to maintain their faith and culture throughout the Ottoman period. To practice their faith, though, they were required to pay the *jizya* in exchange for their *dhimmi* status. Some who were unable to afford it, converted to Islam to escape the *jizya*. They also faced restrictions on public displays of religion, the construction of new churches, and participation in political or military leadership.

The Ottoman period marked a significant change in the way the Jewish community was treated in Lebanon. While maintaining the *dhimmi* system and requiring the *jizya*, the Ottomans granted the Jewish community a more structured form of self-governance through the millet system. Jewish religious practices were largely permitted, with active synagogues and schools. The community was granted a degree of autonomy, especially in matters of religious law, which were overseen by Jewish religious leaders. During this time, Lebanon became a crucial part of the Mediterranean trade network, with Jewish communities playing an essential role, particularly in the trade of textiles and silk.

By the 16th century, Lebanon was already home to diverse religious communities, especially in coastal cities that had accepted Christianity since its inception. Not much later, Mount Lebanon had also accepted Christianity early in similar ways as the coast. In addition, conversions had taken place through the work of disciples of Saint Maron even before his followers migrated to Mount Lebanon after his death, resulting in a prominent presence for Christians, a majority of whom were Maronites, throughout its regions. Sunni communities were also well-established in Beirut,

Sidon, and Tripoli. The Shia communities had strong presence in the mountainous regions of Jabal Amel, the Beqaa Valley, and parts of Mount Lebanon. The Druze were also well-established there, with a significant presence in the Chouf area of Mount Lebanon and Wadi al-Taym area of Mount Hermon. And, the smaller Jewish communities was predominantly living in major coastal cities, primarily Beirut and Sidon.

From the mid-1500s to the early 1800s, the Ottoman Caliphate granted Mount Lebanon some degree of self-rule, often shared between the two main communities living there: Christians and Druze. This arrangement, while not always, generally favored the Druze. As was the case under the rule of earlier Caliphates, the Church was able to play a central role in preserving the religious and cultural identity of Lebanese Christians. The Maronite Patriarch acted as both a spiritual leader and a civic leader, often negotiating with the Ottomans on behalf of his people. He also maintained strong ties with European powers, particularly France and the Vatican. These ties provided diplomatic protection, even though the Ottomans persecuted Christians during periods of political instability or European intervention.

A Period of Expansion in the Christian Communities in Lebanon

The presence of Christians in Lebanon up until this period can be attributed to two primary reasons. First, the conversions that took place during the early period of Christianity throughout the Land of Canaan, but especially in Lebanon's coastal cities initially and then later in the mountains. Second, a subsequent migration occurred of Syriac Christians from the Antioch area to Mount Lebanon, including the followers of Saint Maron, who joined existing Christians already living there, including Maronites, sharing their faith and culture. Additionally, continuous conversions took place as a result of the interactions between these Christian communities and other communities living there, notably polytheists. Subsequently, persistent migration waves from various parts of the Levant also occurred under the reign of the different Muslim Caliphates as well as during those of Crusaders, but to a lesser extent. It is important to note, though, that more systematic migration waves occurred during the Ottoman rule.

The resulting Christian communities in Lebanon, their cultures, practices, traditions, and affiliations evolved as a consequence of the numerous schisms, whether within the Church of Antioch itself or within the wider Christian Church, impacting the nomenclatures and realignments of the different groups.

The presence of Greek Orthodox in Lebanon, for example, has Antiochene and Byzantine roots. The Greek influence on Lebanese culture and religion goes back to ancient times when the Lebanese coast was Hellenized by Alexander the Great. This influence only grew under the Byzantine Empire. Furthermore, an influx of Greek Orthodox arrived in Lebanon from nearby parts of the Levant when it fell under the Arab conquests. In addition to many coastal cities, but primarily Beirut, Greek Orthodox settled in various areas of the mountains and Eastern Lebanon, including Akkar, Koura, Jbeil, Matn, Baabda, Aley, Zahle, Hasbaya, Marjaayoun, and the Beqaa, among others.

It is difficult to separate the original presence and subsequent migration of Greek Catholics, namely the Melkites, also Antiochene, in Lebanon from that of the Greek Orthodox. This is so because until the 18th century, when Melkites separated from the Orthodox Church, they were united in one community. However, starting about that time, many Melkite families and communities living in Syria migrated to Lebanon to join the existing Melkite community in Beirut and various parts of Mount Lebanon as well as other coastal and Eastern areas of today's Lebanon including Zahle, Matn, Chouf, Jezzine, Sidon, Tyre, and Baalbek.

Armenian migration to Lebanon also began toward the end of the 17th century, occurring in waves. Initially, like other Christians, Armenians were fleeing the harsh conditions of living under Ottoman rule into the security of the semi-autonomous regions of Lebanon. Subsequent migration intensified, which became forced displacement during and after the Armenian Genocide that began in 1915 and lasted beyond the end of the First World War. Armenians arriving in Lebanon settled primarily in Beirut, Matn, Anjar, and the Beqaa. Like the Canaanites, the Armenians were also early Christians. In fact, Armenia adopted Christianity as a state religion in 301. The majority of Armenian Christians in Lebanon belong to the Armenian Apostolic Church, an Orthodox community formed in 610. However, the Armenian Catholic Church was later formed, in 1742, which is headquartered in Lebanon.

The Syriac Orthodox migration to Lebanon, also with Antiochene roots, began in the 17th century, when the Jacobites formed their first community in Tripoli. Additional waves of Syriac Orthodox migration followed periodically and continued throughout the 20th century, resulting in their heavy presence in Beirut and Zahle.

It is even more difficult to separate the original presence and subsequent migration of Syriac Catholics in Lebanon from that of the Syriac Orthodox as the two were one community until their initial split in 1677, which was interrupted and did not go into full effect until 1782, and has remained so until the present time. Despite the split, the two small groups remained a tightly coupled community.

The exact start of the migration period of Copts to Lebanon is not as clear as it is for other Christian sects. However, there is evidence of historic Coptic presence in Lebanon as early as the Fatimid period, when they migrated in search of religious freedom. Additional Coptic migration took place under the Crusaders when Egypt was under the Ayyubid rule. The rise of sectarian tensions during certain periods of the Ottoman reign led more Copts to Lebanon.

The most recent addition to the Lebanese Christian communities were the Protestants. The Protestant Reformation of 1517, essentially a major schism in the Western Church, challenged the Catholic Church's practices and led to new Christian denominations. Although a small number of Protestants came to Lebanon from nearby Levant regions, the majority were converted by British and American missionaries, starting in the 19th century. The small community of Lebanese Protestants is today centered in Beirut.

CHAPTER 13.

Christian-Druze Self-Rule in Mount Lebanon

CHRISTIANS AND DRUZE IN MOUNT Lebanon coexisted relatively peacefully under the leadership of ruthless centralized rulers and ineffectual local leaders. Despite serious external and internal challenges faced by these communities, at times leading to unfortunate and destructive strife between them, they formed mutually beneficial alliances as they sought and protected autonomy for themselves in the Lebanese mountains. This self-rule in Mount Lebanon, negotiated with the Ottomans, allowed for local leaders to rise to power under the title of emirs, or princes. Two families in particular, the Maans (1516-1697) and the Chehabs (1697-1842), or Shihabs, played significant roles in that regard. In reality, the Maan and Chehab families governed Mount Lebanon as tax collectors for the Ottomans rather than as independent royalty or autonomous rulers. There were also other regional local feudal lords, from prominent families of all religious groups, who were influential with, but subservient to, the emirs and Ottoman rulers.

The Maans

The Maans, a Druze family of the Southern Arabian Banu Maan tribe that migrated to Lebanon in the 12th century, had its sphere of influence in the Chouf district of Mount Lebanon, and managed to establish an influential rule over Lebanon, especially under the leadership of Emir Fakhreddine II (1590-1635), the most prominent Maan ruler. Initially, Baakline was the center of their power, but Fakhr-al-Din II moved to Deir el Qamar, both in the Chouf, which became the new seat for their rule. Fakhreddine II, the grandson of another strong leader, Fakhreddine I, was a skilled leader, and desired to establish an independent principality in the mountains while managing to satisfy both Christians and Druze. He also forged important relations with European royalty, especially the Grand Duke of Tuscany. After a period of exile in Tuscany, as a result of his disputes with the Ottomans, he returned to Mount Lebanon and rebuilt his power base, including in the majority Christian parts of the principality. However, the Ottomans became suspicious again of his appealing style of leadership and growing power, ultimately arresting and exiling him to Istanbul, where he was killed in 1635. This was one of the reasons that the Maans' rule weakened and eventually contributed to bringing an end to it.

The Chehabs

The Chehabs were originally a Sunni family, with kinship relations with the Maan Druze family, but some of their ruling members converted to Christianity. They also originally hailed from the Banu Shihab Arab tribe from the Hejaz, settled in the Houran region on the border of Syria and Jordan, then migrated to Wadi al-Taym in South Lebanon in the 12th century. In 1697, the Maan family was left without a willing or able male heir to continue their rule and thus opted to nominate an emir who is a relative of theirs, Bashir, from the Chehab family and whose mother was a Maan. His immediate successor, Haydar, was also the son of a Druze mother, although he worked to severely reduce the Druze's influence and grip on power in Mount Lebanon. Initially, the Chehabs ruled Lebanon by working closely with the Ottomans as they continued to manage local autonomy. The Chehabs' most significant ruler would not emerge though until the reign of Emir Bashir II (1788-1840). By then, his branch of the family had adopted a new religion, Maronite Christianity. Thus, Bachir II served in his princely role as a Christian, working closely with the Maronite Church. Under his leadership, while also continuing to erode the power of Druze feudal lords, the Chehabs controlled much of Lebanon, uniting the different regions and growing their own influence.

Bashir II also built and moved the court to Beiteddine Palace. Eventually, his rule was mired by conflicts between the Druze and Christians, and he shifted his support from the Ottomans to a local Egyptian ruler, which led to the demise of his reign. Despite his significance and earlier success, he became unpopular and faced a rebellion in 1840 due to his alliance with Egypt's ruler, who had invaded Lebanon. As a result, the Ottomans appointed Bashir bin Qasim bin Melhem al-Chehab, or Bashir III, but did so without consulting anyone in Mount Lebanon, especially Christian and Druze leaders, which constituted a departure from the norm. This appointment further aggravated the situation among all impacted parties, compelling the Ottomans to abruptly end Bashir's rule in 1842; thus, his reign lasted for only two years. The confluence of these developments ended the Chehabs' rule permanently when the Ottoman Sultan, aiming to regain control of a volatile situation, appointed Omar Pasha, a Serbian convert to Islam, as Governor of Mount Lebanon.

External Challenges—Egypt's Invasion

While still a part of the Ottoman Caliphate, Egypt had remained semi-autonomous due to the lingering influence of the Mamluks. In 1805, Muhammad Ali Pasha took control and sought to make Egypt more independent. He went to war with the Ottomans twice in the 19th century. One of these wars, led by his son, Ibrahim Pasha, impacted Lebanon. In 1831, Ibrahim Pasha invaded Lebanon as a result of a conflict between Muhammad Ali and the Ottoman Sultan. Ibrahim Pasha's troops managed to capture important parts of Lebanon, including coastal cities. He similarly controlled important cities in Palestine and Syria. Even though Ibrahim Pasha controlled Lebanon for only nine years, he put in place harsh measures including high taxes, land confiscation, disarmament, and conscription, impacting both Christians and Druze.

The Christians were disconcerted as they had always feared conscription and struggled with higher taxes. However, the Druze were much more impacted by the Egyptians' rule because many more of them were feudal lords while many of the Christians were farmers. In addition, Ibrahim Pasha marginalized the Druze by shifting much of the tax collection responsibility to the Christians, tipping the balance of power in their favor, which further contributed to a growing Christian-Druze environment of mutual distrust, eventually leading to adversarial relations. Universally despised, Ibrahim Pasha was eventually pushed back from Lebanon in 1841 through a revolt conducted by members of all different religious denominations and sects—with the help of an international alliance that included Britain, Austria, Russia, and, of course, the Ottoman Caliphate.

Internal Challenges—The Changing Dynamics of Christian-Druze Relations

Helping the Mamluks fight against the Crusaders and later supporting the Ottomans in their victory against the Mamluks netted the Druze enormous rewards. By the late 1500s, the Druze became the new feudal lords of Mount Lebanon, enjoying considerable autonomy and great powers through the mid-1800s. Despite this, the Druze would eventually have a change of heart and turn against the Ottomans in search of greater independence, which led to a diminished role for them.

Significantly, when the Druze had the upper hand, there were clashes with the Christians, who had earlier welcomed them and lived side-by-side with them in the mountains, resulting in bloodshed and destruction for both communities. Two noteworthy conflicts serve as important milestones in the relations between the two competing dwellers of Mount Lebanon: the 1840 and 1860 conflicts. Another important clash during this period was with the Ottomans: The Keserwan Peasant Revolt of the late 1850s.

The 1840 Christian-Druze Conflict

This conflict had two root causes, one internal and another external. Internally, at least originally, this discord did not have anything to do with Christian-Druze relations from a religious standpoint. It was essentially a dispute between landowners, generally Druze, and land workers, generally Christian. However, it was fueled, in part, by the Egyptian occupation of Mount Lebanon for nearly a decade. The Christians feared for their safety and autonomy as well as the overall well-being of their community during this period of Egyptian occupation under Muhammad Ali Pasha, who controlled their region as part of his broader territorial expansion against the Ottoman Sultan. Ibrahim Pasha, the son of Muhammad Ali and the effective ruler of Lebanon, had been putting in place new measures to centralize power and reduce the influence of local rule. Christians expressed vehement opposition to Ibrahim Pasha's decision to disarm and then conscript them. The Christians preferred to die in their homeland defending their faith and freedom over dying in a distant land fighting to gain power for the Egyptians or to keep the Ottomans in power.

The situation in Mount Lebanon became a focal point for an internal dispute due to its sectarian dynamics. While the Christians resisted these changes, the Druze divided their loyalties, putting them somewhat at odds with the Christians. True to form, this diversion was exploited by the occupier, leading to a bloody outcome for the residents of Mount Lebanon, from both the Christian and Druze sides. In the end, the Egyptian forces were defeated in

1840, and the region subsequently reverted to Ottoman control. The Ottomans then suppressed the conflict with a change in Mount Lebanon governance under pressure from European nations. A serious consequence of this conflict was in how it sowed the seeds for a much bloodier and more destructive conflict a mere two decades later.

The Qaim-Maqamate Provincial System (1843-1861)

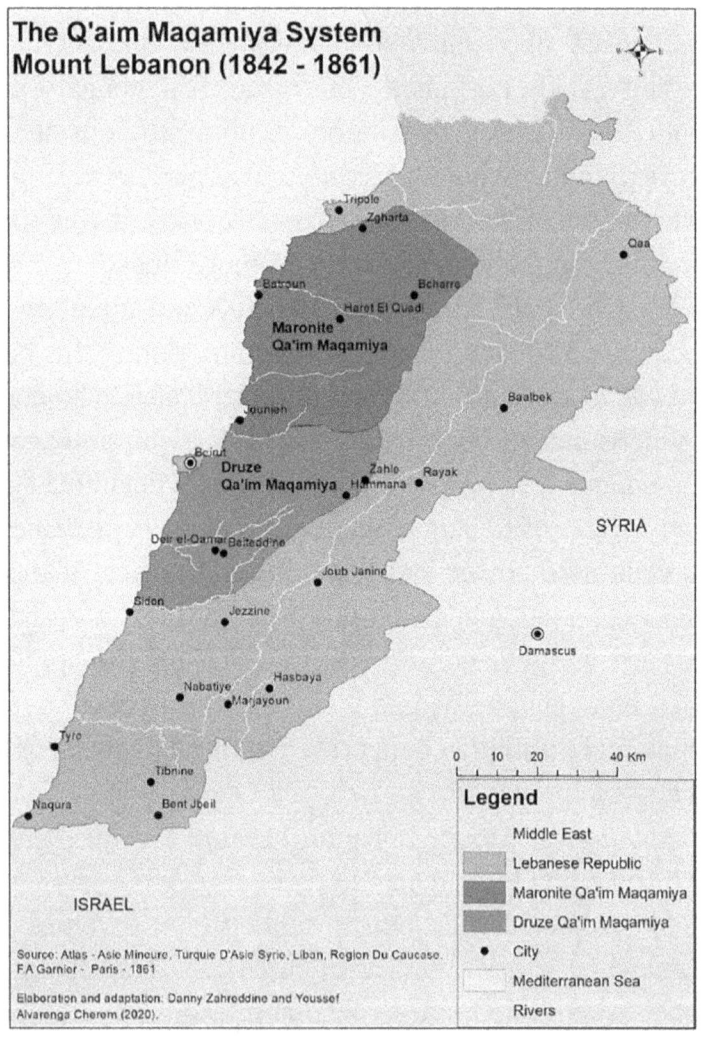

The Qaim Maqamate Provincial System of Mount Lebanon

The first significant conflict between the Christians and Druze in Mount Lebanon, despite their neighborly relations in general, demonstrated that serious tension might arise between them at any time due to political and social circumstances as well as regional events, such as the Egyptian occupation. Bashir II's alliance with the Egyptians and his unpopular decrees regarding the feudal class angered both sides for different reasons and led to a rebellion against him, culminating in violence and carnage. In 1840, he was deposed and replaced by his son as tensions between the Christians and the Druze were escalating, resulting in significant bloodshed. This sectarian violence spread to many areas where the two groups came in contact with each other, reaching a dangerous level and leading to numerous massacres, with many people killed, especially among the Christian population. The Ottoman Caliphate, with prodding from Europeans, especially France, intervened to quell the violence and restore order. The French also pushed the Ottomans to implement a new form of governance that physically and geographically separated the two contentious communities.

Creating two separate districts in Mount Lebanon, a Christian-majority district to the north and a Druze-majority district to the south, was the proposed remedy. This new plan brought an end to the Mount Lebanon Emirate form of government and was seen as an opportunity to create a new system of governance that would allow for addressing the grievances of both sides. The Beirut-Damascus highway served as the dividing line between the two districts. Thus, the Qaim-Maqamate (1843-1861), or provinces, a form of Ottoman indirect rule, was established. This system of local governance essentially required a dual leadership, Qaim-Maqams, to maintain a balanced representation for Christians and Druze and serve as representatives of the local populations to the Ottoman and Christian authorities, ensuring that concerns would be raised and managed. The logic offered by European mediators was that Mount Lebanon was majority Christian but increasingly dominated by Druze under Muslim Caliphates, especially the Ottomans; the two autonomous districts could rebalance the sectarian realities brought on by the successive Arab and Muslim Caliphates. More importantly, Christians believed that local authority would restore a system of governance they had in earlier times, when they had supermajority and significant authority in the mountains, allowing them to manage their affairs more effectively and harmoniously.

Unfortunately, the reality on the ground did not match the theory behind the division on Mount Lebanon and, in fact, seemed to worsen tensions across religious lines despite a dividing boundary. The Druze, unsettled and resentful about their diminished power, and the Christians, with their fears heightened and easily provoked, found themselves mired in more conflicts. These conflicts, at times incited and enabled by Ottoman governors, were increasingly violent, with a significant number of Christians killed.

The 1860 Christian-Druze Conflict

The dual governing system created in 1843 failed to address underlying sectarian tensions. The Ottomans' administrative reform was perceived as challenging Druze dominance and favoring Christians and their European supporters, further deepening the divide. Under more autonomy, however, the Christians were able to establish themselves in trade and commerce, reclaiming their economic and political assertiveness. These new realities increased resentment that continued to escalate due to the persistent sectarian divide, socioeconomic disparities, and competing nationalistic aspirations.

The Ottomans, using their divide-and-conquer strategy at every possible opportunity, showed their ingenuity in exploiting the religious and sociopolitical differences between the Christians and the Druze and fanning it into violent sectarian disputes. Even minor incidents easily escalated into widespread fighting. While the leadership of the two communities tried to mitigate conflicts, with time, disagreements between the Christians and Druze were becoming increasingly frequent and more violent.

The Christian-Druze conflict of 1860 was a tipping point, an all-out battle resulting in devastation to the Christian communities, with massacres in numerous Christian regions leading to the deaths of some ten thousand Christians, with many fleeing survivors mercilessly and fatally attacked by Ottomans. Under attack with many of their villages burnt, the Christians, who were initially in a defense mode, subsequently went on the offense on a number of fronts. However, with support from some local Ottoman officials, the Druze had the upper hand. The conflict spread across Mount Lebanon and parts of Syria, where massacres of Christians occurred as well, further alarming European powers.

With thousands of Christians killed and an even larger number injured and many of their villages totally destroyed, the Druze moved quickly to assert their control over the additional territory they gained as the Christians retreated into safer areas of their semi-autonomous enclave of Mount Lebanon. As many Christians became isolated, and others living in fragmented areas in Mount Lebanon, the Druze enjoyed increased dominance. Another important development, as a result of this conflict, is that Mount Lebanon was placed under the direct rule of Ottoman authority in Damascus, instead of the Ottoman ruler in Sidon, who also resided in Beirut. This move was, at least, seen as a symbolic loss of autonomy for Mount Lebanon. The conflict of 1860 between Christians and Druze was not isolated to only Mount Lebanon. It spread to other areas of Lebanon, including the Beqaa and Jabal Amel, becoming a wider Christian-Muslim conflict. Intervention by France, again, compelled the Ottoman Caliphate to restore order.

This uncertain period of conflict between the Christians and Druze marked the beginning of the Lebanese Christian emigration, this time primarily to the West. The first Lebanese immigrant arrived in the United States in 1854, the beginning of an exodus that intensified in the decades leading up to and following the First World War. However, some people opted to stay close to the homeland and preferred to emigrate to Egypt, at least initially. Although Egypt was also under the Ottoman Caliphate's rule, it was enjoying a robust autonomy under Muhammad Ali Pasha. The majority of these Christians belonged to the Melkite Greek Catholic and Greek Orthodox denominations, although some Maronites also followed suit.

The Keserwan Revolt in Mount Lebanon

Burdened by taxes imposed by the Ottoman Caliphate, collected through local rulers, the Christians began to openly revolt against their rulers in the early 1800s, demanding the abolishment of the feudal class and its practices. At the same time, the Christians were aggrieved over the Druzes' leveraging of their religion with the Ottomans to gain the political upper hand, even though the Druze did not share the Sunni Muslim adherence. For the first time since the seventh century, the Christians in Lebanon, and specifically in Mount Lebanon, where they had felt fortified and protected, felt vulnerable. This time, their opponents were not invaders but neighbors sharing the mountains with them.

The Keserwan Revolt in Mount Lebanon, a series of event between 1858 and 1861, was led by Tanious Shahin, a Christian peasant who revolted against heavy taxation and exploitation by feudal landlords. Such Christian protests had been going on since the early 1800s for a number of reasons. The most significant revolts occurred around 1821 against Emir Bashir's taxation policies; in 1840 against conscription; and in 1858 against feudal practices, among many other reasons. These rebellions were referred to as "*ammiyyat,*" a word that has its roots in "*amma,*" or commoners.

The Keserwan Peasant Revolt was the most successful of these rebellions, aiming to end the hereditary privileges of the feudal class that controlled Mount Lebanon. These families, at the time, were acting as tax collectors on behalf of Emir Bashir Chehabi II, who was remitting the taxes to the Ottoman rulers in return for protecting his princely privileges and who had managed to suppress earlier uprisings. Shahin, working with and acting on behalf of other peasants, demanded that the feudal class relinquish its privileges. They refused, but in the end the peasants of Mount Lebanon prevailed and were able to eventually obtain concessions from the landlords, including land ownership and political representation for themselves. The 1860 Christian-Druze conflict and, to some extent, the Keserwan revolt led to the formation of yet a new form of governance: the Mount Lebanon Mutasarrifate, in 1861.

The Mutasarrifate Provincial System (1861-1918)

The earlier Qaim-Maqamate system of governance, put in place in 1843, did not improve the relations between the Christians and the Druze as had been hoped. In fact, their differences seemed to increase and bring more agitation, culminating with the conflict of 1860. That was serious enough to bring an end to the Qaim-Maqamate.

With European mediation, and especially active involvement by the French, the Mount Lebanon Mutasarrifate, another form of Ottoman indirect rule, was created in 1861. This semi-autonomous governance model, under a non-Lebanese Christian governor who was appointed directly by the Ottoman central authorities with European approval, provided an increased measure of stability and a degree of autonomy for the Christians. In fact, under the Christian-majority Mount Lebanon Mutasarrifate, Lebanon experienced relative peace as the French maintained close relations with the Christian population, particularly the Maronites.

Even though the overall situation remained fragile, with the religious balance constantly shifting, the Christians were able to experience a greater degree of religious and political stability. More importantly, the relative peace allowed all Lebanese to benefit from investments in critical infrastructure including railroads,

roads, and port facilities. Economic growth followed, making Lebanon a center for trade, particularly between Europe and the Middle East. Education, at all levels, received increased internal and external interest. Higher learning institutions such as the American University of Beirut, established in 1866, and the Jesuit Saint Joseph University, established in 1875, contributed to a cultural and intellectual renaissance in Lebanon and the region.

While this new form of government constituted some semblance of an early homeland for the Christians that would later follow, it was one that entrenched sectarian identities and external influences in Lebanese politics for generations. Perhaps one bright light in this whole situation was the eventual abolishing of the feudal class, and its oppressive taxation system, which had endured for centuries past the time when industrialization rendered it obsolete. This outcome pleased the majority of Christians and a large segment of the Druze population.

The Mount Lebanon Mutasarrifate remained part of Damascus' Ottoman reporting line until 1888, when the Caliphate created the Beirut *Vilayet*, an administrative region extending from Latakia in the north to Jaffa in the south, essentially covering most of the Levant's Mediterranean coast. Although it was made part of Beirut *Vilayet*, which made sense geographically, the Mount Lebanon Mutasarrifate was able to keep its already existing distinct autonomy and administrative structure, headed by a governor who was appointed directly by, and reported to, the Ottoman central government. Except for the Mount Lebanon Mutasarrifate, these regions had been governed as part of the Syria *Vilayet*, established in 1865. The Ottomans' aim from this restructuring was to improve administrative efficiency and assert greater control over Beirut, which was becoming an economic and trade focal point between the Near East and Europe. The inclusion of Mount Lebanon in this new *Vilayet*, or administrative structure, was in response to increased pressure by France on the Ottomans to ensure harmony in Mount Lebanon and to continue to manage sectarian tensions.

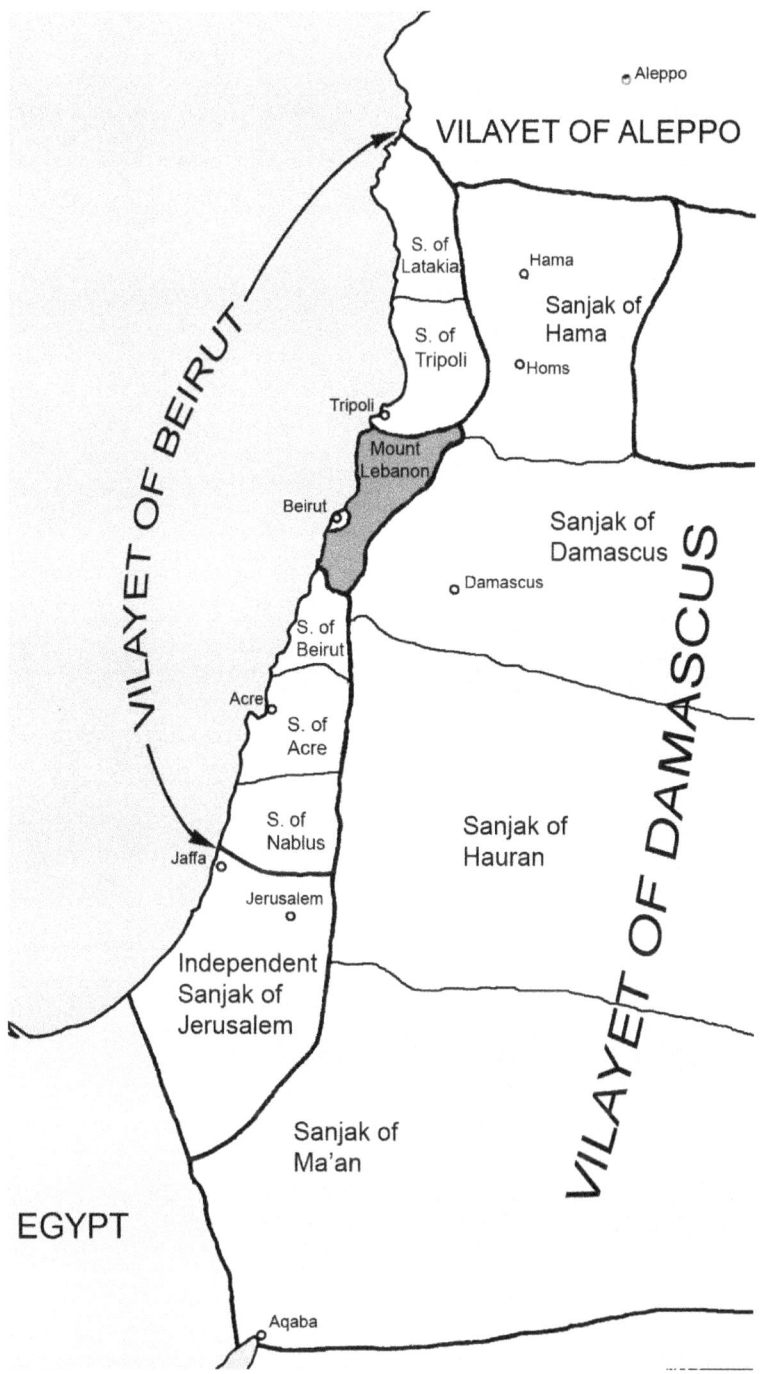

Vilayet of Beirut Under the Ottomans

CHAPTER 14.

The Realities of War, Famine, and Emigration

The Ottoman Caliphate suffered a series of defeats all over its occupied territories in Europe, Asia, and Africa towards the end of the 19th century, which left it both militarily and economically weakened, earning it the nickname "sick man" of Europe. The continued strengthening of the British Empire and the emergence of Germany, France, and Russia as regional powers was already changing the international realities. It did not take long for another war to start, this time on a much larger scale.

The First World War

The war began in 1914, and it involved the Ottoman Caliphate fighting on the side of the Central Powers, alongside Germany, Austria-Hungary, and later, Bulgaria, against the Allied Powers of Great Britain, France, Italy, Russia, and Japan, with the United States subsequently joining in. The assassination of Archduke Franz Ferdinand of Austria-Hungary may have given it the impetus to start but, in reality, the First World War was caused by a transformation taking place in a more confident and assertive Europe, strengthened by these alliances, as well as rising nationalism and an appetite for imperialism.

Lebanon was intensely impacted because the Ottoman Caliphate's primary theater of operations was in the Near and

Middle East. Major battles also took place in the Caucasus, the Balkans, and Asia Minor. The Ottomans battled primarily Great Britain, France, and Russia in these areas. While this resulted in the natural easing of their grip in many places, it also led to some desperate and extreme measures on the Ottomans' part in these same places in order to keep control, including Lebanon. Sensing the looming troubles for Istanbul and its Sultan, the regional Ottoman rulers were too quick to hand out harsh sentences, collective and individual, such as the burning of harvests and the hanging of Lebanese who were active in freedom movements, to enforce their dominance and stamp out the rising freedom movements.

The Ottoman Caliphate collapsed in 1918, and Lebanon was placed under the League of Nations' French Mandate for Syria and Lebanon. Preparing for this day, Britain and France had already, in 1916, secretly agreed to divide, between the two of them, the Ottoman territory in the Near and Middle East into different spheres of influence. This arrangement, the Sykes-Picot Agreement, gave France control over Lebanon and Syria. Separately, the British played a pivotal role in shaping the Middle East's geography and society through the 1917 Balfour Declaration. In a letter from the British Foreign Secretary, Arthur Balfour, to a leader in the British Jewish community, Lord Rothschild, the government of Britain pledged support for "the establishment in Palestine of a national home for the Jewish people." This promise later became part of the British Mandate for Palestine (1923-1948).

The Jewish community, though relatively small compared to other groups at the onset of the Muslim conquest, had a continuous presence in Lebanon for over two millennia, enduring well into the establishment of modern Lebanon.

The Locust Plague of 1915

Centuries earlier, the Christians in Mount Lebanon had developed a robust organization to manage their internal affairs and meet their communal needs, including self-sustaining farming. This allowed them to endure the difficult times they experienced under the Arab conquests and Muslim Caliphates. However, in 1915, a drought and a locust plague exacerbated the situation and decimated Mount Lebanon's nascent agricultural base. By this point, local communities had little, if any, access to food or resources. As the war progressed, the Ottoman military, concerned with the impact of food scarcity on its own forces, imposed stringent controls on the sale and transport of essential grains, such as wheat and barley. These measures intensified the dire food shortages, transforming the crisis into a full-blown famine.

The aftermath of the locust infestation lingered because it disrupted expected yields from all kinds of crops, annuals and perennials, and trees, which made it impossible to have new rounds of planting and harvesting since few or no seeds were produced. Thus, the famine resulted in ongoing and widespread malnutrition, which precipitated a public health catastrophe. Diseases spread rapidly among the population. The suffering, starvation, and death that ensued as a result of the cruel Ottoman policies during the conflict, which aggravated the effects of the locust plague, became a grim daily reality for many Christians in Lebanon.

The Great Famine of Mount Lebanon

The Great Famine of Mount Lebanon (1915-1918) is a tragic episode of starvation that led to the death of more than 200,000 individuals in the semi-autonomous region, a mortality rate higher than that experienced in any other Ottoman territory during the First World War because of the Ottomans' misguided policies. Naval operations and blockades in the Eastern Mediterranean, enforced by both sides of the warring powers, prevented any form of aid from arriving in Mount Lebanon and its coastal region.

At the start of the war, the Ottoman authorities were concerned about the potential for French and British intervention along the

Eastern Mediterranean and thus rushed to put in place a naval blockade along the Lebanese coast. Furthermore, the Ottomans were especially concerned about the prospect of Christian cooperation with any potential European intervention, which could weaken the Ottomans and facilitate the Christians' inclination to pursue any possible open path for their freedom. Similarly, starting in 1915, in order to deprive the Ottoman Caliphate of goods and supplies, the Allied powers enforced their own blockade of the Eastern Mediterranean using their naval assets.

This complex geopolitical-religious situation had an adverse effect on the Lebanese Christians who, by then, had indeed developed even stronger European ties, especially with France. More importantly, the Lebanese Christians, sensing cracks in the iron grip of the Ottomans, certainly saw an opportunity to fight for their freedom. To preempt this, the Ottoman military trampled on the semi-autonomous status of Mount Lebanon with a series of direct interventions including the deployment of their own forces to the region early in the war. By far the most devastating measure, though, was the Ottomans' intentional restriction of access to Mount Lebanon, in addition to the blockade enforced by the Allied powers. The Ottomans cordoned off the mountains from surrounding regions as part of their own broader blockade of the Eastern Mediterranean region. This isolation, coupled with the punitively restrictive access to the Beqaa Valley and the confiscation of essential goods, precipitated an acute food shortage.

In the end, close to half the population of Mount Lebanon—estimated at around 100,000 to 150,000 people—succumbed to famine and starvation caused by the confluence of drought and locust infestation that started in 1915. This crisis was further aggravated by naval blockades of the Lebanese coast and the Ottomans' purposeful besiegement of Mount Lebanon, which lasted until the end of the war. In 1916, the total population of Mount Lebanon was estimated to be between 300,000 and 400,000 people.

An Intense Period of Suffering and Death Leads to Emigration

In the aftermath of the 1840 and 1860 Christian-Druze conflicts, before it was even evident that a world war would soon commence, the Christians' feeling of vulnerability turned into real fear of potential recurrences of similar massacres. Furthermore, growing troubles for the Ottoman Caliphate in distant lands made the omnipresent threat of conscription of Lebanese Christians into the armed forces of the Ottoman Empire even greater. Geographically isolated into mainly rugged and remote parts of Mount Lebanon, cut off from contacts with other Christian communities in the region suffering similar hardships, and continuing clashes with neighboring Druze made some Christians contemplate their future in farther, but safer, lands. Accordingly, an emigration wave began, starting in 1854, between the two famed Christian-Druze conflicts, that would continue into the present time.

The Christians' feelings of vulnerability and their desire to escape from the insecurity that unsettled them continued to gain momentum and intensify. Thus, the periods leading up to, during, and right after the First World War, which included the disease, crop devastation, and forced hunger experienced by the Lebanese, naturally led to more emigration. By the end of the First World War, nearly one-quarter of Mount Lebanon's population was lost to emigration.

As the Ottoman Caliphate reached its final days, Mount Lebanon seemed on the brink of extinction in so many ways, most notably demographically. Nearly three-quarters of its population, or up to 300,000 of an estimated 400,000 people, was lost to death and emigration during the last half-century of Ottoman rule. In 1918, at the war's conclusion, entire villages in Lebanon were left depopulated, with many reduced to ghost towns, standing as vivid evidence of famine, disease, death, and intensifying emigration.

CHAPTER 15.

Reaffirming the Homeland—At the Versailles Conference

WITH THE COLLAPSE OF THE Ottoman Caliphate at the end of the First World War in 1918, Lebanon was placed under the League of Nations' French Mandate for Syria and Lebanon. With already strong ties to France, the Christians emerged from the war as a politically influential group. Seen as an advocate for religious coexistence in Lebanon and a catalyst for change, in 1919, members of the Lebanese communities delegated Maronite Patriarch Elias Peter Hoayek to represent their aspirations for an independent Lebanon in a memorandum to the Paris Peace Conference, also known as the Versailles Conference. A year later, in 1920, the state of Greater Lebanon was proclaimed by the French.

After centuries of oppression and violence, the Christians were exhausted but not broken. The attempt by the last Caliphate to erase the Lebanese identity had failed, and the Ottoman Caliphate itself was abolished in 1922, although in reality their reign ended in 1918. The transition from Ottoman rule to the French Mandate fundamentally changed the social and economic landscape of Lebanon, setting the stage for the eventual creation of the modern Lebanese state. The Christians played a leading role in shaping the political and cultural landscape of this new state.

With the channels of communication, in many forms, reopened between Lebanon and the rest of the world, the situation began to improve. Funds sent into Lebanon by concerned Lebanese immigrants eager to help their loved ones enabled the country and its weary citizens to begin recovering, slowly but steadily, from a long, deadly, and destructive period into normalcy and prosperity. Although the French, who had played an important role in the Crusades, had not managed to liberate the Holy Land centuries before, they returned to Lebanon in 1920 with an official mandate. For the first time in probably centuries, the Christians of Lebanon felt safer in their homeland, with new boundaries and a new name.

Grand Liban

On September 1, 1920, the French announced the creation of Grand Liban, or Greater Lebanon, expanding the semi-autonomous Mutasarrifate of Mount Lebanon to encompass new areas of diverse religious makeup, including the largest coastal cities of Beirut, Tripoli, Sidon, Tyre, as well as the Beqaa Valley.

In 1926, Lebanon elected its first president, Charles Debbas, an Orthodox Christian, with all subsequent presidents from that point on being Maronites, as dictated by the new Lebanese Constitution. In the meanwhile, those who had left Lebanon were still feeling connected to their former homeland, sending funds routinely to their families in Lebanon. More importantly, this was a period of relative peace and harmony that saw many of these immigrants coming back into the country. The infusion of hard-earned money from abroad as well as education and expertise gained by the returning Lebanese immigrants marked a point in Lebanon's modern history when the country began to build its necessary civic systems, public infrastructure, business networks, and educational institutions, among the many additional components necessary for the evolution of a modern society.

While many of these institutions would continue to suffer severe setbacks due to more wars and violence in Lebanon and that part of the world, the influx of resources and expertise from Lebanese living and working abroad into their home country has remained an important source of revenue and knowledge for the Lebanese economy that has enabled it to sustain successive conflicts and hardships.

The Republic of Lebanon

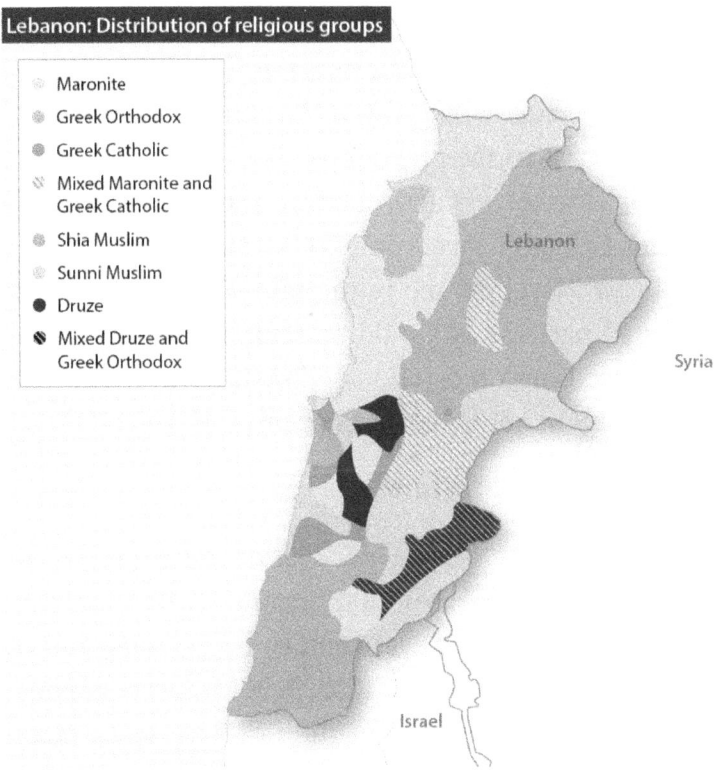

Distribution of Religious Groups in Lebanon

Growing nationalist movements, on both the Christian and Muslim sides, eventually sought independence from French rule, which was granted. Thus, the French Mandate for Lebanon, established under the League of Nations in 1920, came to its natural conclusion in 1943: the Republic of Lebanon, a totally independent state, was born. The demographic change resulting from the establishment of Grand Liban created a new reality that called for a governance system based on the country's diverse sectarian representation, which gave rise to an unwritten National Pact. This understanding between the main religious denominations of Lebanon was a political power-sharing arrangement that allocated governance responsibilities among Lebanon's various religious sects.

An important foundation for the Pact was a compromise on the part of the Lebanese. Specifically, the Muslims would relinquish their desire to join in with neighboring Syria or any other Arab nation, and the Christians would forgo Western alliance in choosing to become integral to the creation of modern Lebanon, while maintaining their distinct identity, thereby jointly founding their new independent Lebanon. According to the terms of the Pact, the president would be Maronite, the prime minister would be Sunni, and the speaker of parliament would be Shia. Parliamentary seats were allocated based on a 6:5 ratio of Christians to Muslims, reflecting the Christian majority as per the census of 1932.

The Dual Impact of Emigration

The latter stages of the Ottoman occupation of Lebanon, from the mid-19th century to the early 20th century, were particularly precarious. This is because the last century of Ottoman rule witnessed significant religious and social strife in Mount Lebanon, the Christian hinterland, including persecution that caused a massive Christian exodus from Lebanon into many corners of the world.

The first Lebanese immigrant to the United States arrived in Boston in 1854. He was a Christian from Mount Lebanon whose family had already clashed violently with the Druze. It did not take long before many more Lebanese, especially Christians, migrated out of their homeland in all directions and by all means, some voluntary while others were forced. They sought better and safer lives in faraway countries and continents. North and South America were favored destinations, but equally large numbers went to Australia. Since Lebanon was occupied by the Ottoman Caliphate at the time, Lebanese immigrants to Australia were classified first as Turks, or Syro-Lebanese because, for a period of time under the Ottoman Caliphate, Lebanon and Syria were ruled together as one administrative entity. The designation changed to Lebanese starting in the 1920s after Lebanon, by then already a French protectorate, encompassed Mount Lebanon and surrounding territories.

Ramifications in the New Homelands and Lebanon

The conditions under which most Lebanese emigrated, in large numbers, during this timeframe were horrendous. However, the impact of this exodus has had positive ramifications for the Lebanese abroad and their descendants, for their host communities, and for the Lebanese at home. Initially, the most desired destination for the Christians of Mount Lebanon was the United States of America, and to a lesser extent Canada and Australia. However, many people ended up in Latin America, including Mexico, Brazil, Argentina, Venezuela, Colombia, and Chile. Some also made their way to other South American countries such as Ecuador, Paraguay, Peru, and Uruguay. And a smaller number landed in the Caribbean, including Cuba, the Dominican Republic, and Jamaica. It is estimated that hundreds of thousands of Christians left Mount Lebanon and other parts of today's Lebanon between 1850 and 1920. Despite this mass departure, the 1914 Ottoman census showed about a half million residents of Mount Lebanon, of whom the overwhelming majority were Christian.

Prior to this, the West had not been a destination for the general population except for the small number of Maronite clergy who were routinely sent by the Church to study at the Pontifical Maronite College of Rome and then returned to Mount Lebanon.

The work undertaken by returning clergy has had important and lasting cultural benefits in Lebanon, especially in the domain of education.

Similar benefits, but on a larger scale, were realized with the arrival of other Christian clergy—European Catholic and American Protestant missions—aiming to establish their organizations' presence in the form of schools, healthcare facilities, and printing presses throughout the country. Two of the most visible institutions founded were the American University of Beirut in 1866 and the French Saint Joseph University in 1875, both comprehensive universities with medical schools and hospitals. Even though the Lebanese had grown accustomed to having foreigners in their land, this time these visitors did not come as conquerors or warriors, but instead as bearers of services, ideas, and knowledge to disseminate. Consequently, the increased level of interaction and the resulting positive experiences between the Lebanese and the Western missions further heightened the locals' interest in life abroad.

The Long Road Ahead

Not surprisingly, and as was the case for many other immigrants before them, the early Lebanese immigrants faced difficult conditions in their new homelands. To begin with, they lacked the language skills and were unfamiliar with the Western lifestyle and culture. Most significantly, these immigrants, who were primarily farmers in their old homeland, did not have employable skills fit for the economies of their new homelands. Because of this, Lebanese immigrants turned to peddling, an occupation that required hard work and willingness to travel, usually by horse and carriage but sometimes by foot. In America, it is known that the overwhelming majority of new Lebanese immigrants became peddlers who trekked across the country offering their products door to door, in small towns and large urban centers. With their background as farmers in the harsh and remote hills of Mount Lebanon, and the courage to move so far away from their original homes, such requirements must not have seemed daunting to them.

Hard work, however, did not always guarantee social acceptance. The early wave of Lebanese immigrants was subjected to prejudices and discrimination in their new homelands, not unlike immigrants of many other nations. The most severe form of this was the White Australia policy of the 19th century, which did not change until 1920. This act classified Lebanese immigrants as non-white and thus excluded them from citizenship, the right to vote, and therefore hindered employment. However, despite some discrimination, like most immigrants endured in the United States, the Lebanese were officially included in the Caucasian racial category in the census from the early days, seen then as an advantage. Along with their success in education, medicine, business, and government, this racial classification helped them integrate more readily into American society and facilitated their joining the middle- and upper-class ranks.

Focusing on What Matters

As has always been the case, faith came first for the Lebanese, from their roots in the Levant and Antioch to their new homelands across the globe. The desire to preserve their religious and cultural characteristics prompted the Lebanese Christians, of the various Antiochene churches, to build their own churches, schools, social centers, and even hospitals. The first Maronite church in the US was built in 1887 in Philadelphia. The first Greek Orthodox church was built in 1895 in New York City. The first Greek Catholic Melkite church was built in 1906 in La Crosse, Wisconsin. The first Lebanese church in Australia was established by the Melkite Catholics in 1895, followed by a Maronite church in 1897. The Orthodox built their church in Melbourne in 1931.

The diligence and industriousness of many Lebanese peddlers and merchants allowed them to gradually climb the social and economic ladder, becoming businessmen, wholesalers, owners of department stores, and manufacturers. Evolving from their peddling experience, they owned and operated a large number of silk factories by the 1920s but also expanded their sphere to include banking and finance, creating a Manhattan-based bank as early as the 1890s and forming social and political organizations as early as 1911. As Lebanese immigrants diversified their trade activities and earned a presence in many fields of the country's economic structure, many of them became wealthy.

Success of the Lebanese in their New Homelands

Countless descendants of Lebanese immigrants have made significant contributions across various fields, including government, medicine, and the arts. Their achievements reflect a legacy of excellence and resilience. They placed a strong emphasis on education and hard work as the means of upward mobility, enabling their descendants to join the middle and upper classes.

In the United States, individuals of Lebanese descent have held prominent positions in government, serving as senators, governors, cabinet members, and even presidential candidates. Their leadership and advocacy have left a lasting impact on public policy and governance. In the field of medicine, descendants of Lebanese immigrants have pioneered groundbreaking innovations, particularly in cardiac surgery, revolutionizing medical practices and saving countless lives. Their contributions have earned global recognition and have cemented their place in the history of medical advancements. The arts and literature have also been enriched by the talents of Lebanese immigrants and their descendants. One notable figure, Khalil Gibran, who emigrated with his family in 1895 from the town of Bsharri, a remote region in the northern part of Mount Lebanon, to Boston, a major city in Massachusetts, became a celebrated literary and artistic voice. His works, which explore themes of love, spirituality, and the human connection, continue to inspire readers worldwide.

In Latin America, Lebanese immigrants and their descendants have thrived, achieving remarkable success in business and government. In several countries, they have risen to the highest levels of elective office, including presidencies and vice presidencies. Their influence extends beyond politics, as they have played a pivotal role in shaping industries and economies. In some countries, Lebanese immigrants and their descendants became key drivers of industrial growth, owning a significant percentage of businesses by the mid-20th century.

This trend is echoed in many nations, where individuals of Lebanese descent have held leadership roles as vice presidents, governors, and mayors, contributing to the political and economic development of their adopted homelands. In addition to their professional achievements, Lebanese immigrants have made cultural contributions, including the popularization of their cuisine, which has become a beloved part of the culinary landscape in many countries. For instance, in Australia, Lebanese immigrants faced early challenges but were determined to improve their status and were relentless in seeking opportunities. This strategy proved successful, as individuals of Lebanese descent have achieved notable positions in academia, government, and public service, including roles as governors and mayors. Their accomplishments underscore the importance of education and community support in overcoming adversity and achieving success.

Overall, the contributions of Lebanese immigrants and their descendants span continents and disciplines, reflecting their adaptability, perseverance, and commitment to excellence. Their legacy continues to shape societies and inspire future generations.

CHAPTER 16.

Post-Independence Hope and Despair

Lebanon's transformation from a French Mandate to an independent state and the creation of a fragile sectarian political system laid the groundwork for both early successes and eventual collapse.

Lebanon experienced a period of economic prosperity and cultural renewal in the 1950s and early 1960s, often referred to as the Golden Age, when Beirut became a regional hub for higher education, banking, trade, and tourism, earning it the nickname "the Paris of the East." The strong banking industry that developed in Lebanon following the First World War, during the period of the French Mandate, enabled Beirut to become a major financial and commercial hub in the Middle East. This development was largely due to Lebanon's strategic location and relations with the West as well as other key factors such as foreign investment, a highly educated workforce, and political stability.

However, in 1958, Lebanon faced its first major political crisis. This was sparked by regional developments including the formation of the United Arab Republic, a union between Egypt and Syria, and internal circumstances including the rise of Arab nationalism groups dissatisfied by the pro-Western policies of the president at the time, Camille Chamoun, leading to armed clashes. The crisis ended after the election of a new president, Fouad Chehab, who addressed some of the grievances by implementing reforms aimed at modernizing the state and reducing sectarian tension.

The end of the 1960s, however, ushered in increasing political instability and social tensions resulting from the first influx of Palestinian refugees after the 1948 and 1967 Arab-Israeli wars, which altered Lebanon's demographic balance.

The Palestinians in Lebanon

It is difficult to get exact demographic statistics in Lebanon because the country has not conducted an official population census since 1932. The reason relates to sensitivity surrounding sectarian balance, a basis for the country's power-sharing system. Thus, exact statistics for the number of Palestinians living in Lebanon have always been similarly difficult to determine. However, estimates suggest the Palestinian refugee population—both registered and unregistered—reached a peak in the early 1990s, approaching half a million and making up approximately 15 percent of Lebanon's total population at the time.

Some Palestinians have been there since the first influx from Palestine to Lebanon began in 1948. According to the United Nations Relief and Works Agency (UNRWA) for Palestine Refugees in the Near East, roughly half of these refugees live in twelve different refugee camps spread throughout Lebanon. Over the years, many refugees moved out of the camps into residences in the main coastal cities of Lebanon, especially Beirut, Sidon, Tripoli, and Tyre, accounting for the difference between the total number of refugees in camps and those living outside.

The second major influx of Palestinian refugees arrived after the 1967 Arab-Israeli war. Until 1967, the Palestinians lived peacefully in Lebanon. After the Arab-Israeli war of 1967, and with support from some Arab countries, especially Syria, the Palestinians began receiving arms shipments into their camps in Lebanon and soon established training facilities inside the camps as well as in Eastern and Southern parts of Lebanon.

In 1970, another influx of thousands of Palestinian refugees began to arrive in Lebanon from Jordan by way of Syria, this time heavily armed, after an attempt by Palestinian organizations to overthrow the Hashemite monarchy of Jordan. It did not take long before the Palestinian armed presence in Lebanon became a *de facto* state within a state.

The Palestinian presence in Lebanon is indeed mired in hardship. Their living conditions are impoverished, overcrowded, and residents are afforded very limited civil rights as well as infrastructure. Although, as in any sovereign state, the Lebanese government is obliged to assert its sovereignty over the entire country, it does not extend its security oversight to the Palestinian camps. Municipal, educational, health, and social services to the residents in the said camps are the responsibility of UNRWA. In addition, the Palestinians' rights to work and to own property in Lebanon are severely constrained.

The presence of Palestinian refugees in Lebanon has also caused the Lebanese equal hardship and brought the country much violence. Seeking refuge in Lebanon, after the first Israeli-Arab war in 1948, the Palestinians were placed haphazardly in camps in the main cities and also in locations scattered throughout Lebanon, the majority of which lie alongside large urban centers. Lebanon received by far a greater ratio of Palestinians per capita than any other neighboring country. Beginning in 1965, the Palestinian camps in Lebanon, under the auspices of the Palestine Liberation Organization (PLO), became staging bases for operations against Israel from South Lebanon, resulting in Israeli reprisals on Lebanese land. In November 1969, this practice was formalized in an ill-fated memorandum of understanding, known as the Cairo Agreement, which established ground rules under which the guerrilla activities in Lebanon against Israel would be permitted by the

Lebanese government. Furthermore, the full relocation of the PLO leadership to Lebanon in 1971, after the armed conflict between the Jordanian authorities and the PLO, intensified tensions and increased sectarian polarization.

The text of the Cairo Agreement was never officially published by either side. However, the Agreement, which was divulged by the Lebanese press, essentially purported to regulate the Palestinian presence and their activities in Lebanon at the same time as it placed all Palestinian camps outside the jurisdiction of the Lebanese government. In reality, the Cairo Agreement officially forced Lebanon to acknowledge a sanctioned Palestinian guerrilla war with Israel on Lebanese soil, leading to clashes with the Lebanese Armed Forces, including a major conflict with the Lebanese Army in 1973. More seriously, this effectively breached the armistice treaty signed between Lebanon and Israel in 1949, thus dragging Lebanon into a series of devastating conflicts with Israel. This situation—as well as the inability of the Lebanese government to address a host of deep-seated social, economic, political, and security issues—combined with regional pressures, ultimately led to a total destabilization of the country and brought it to the brink of a civil war in 1975, a bloody and destructive conflict that took on a life of its own and lasted until 1990, with its damaging ramifications continuing to reverberate to this day.

In 1987, the Lebanese government unilaterally nullified the Cairo Agreement. Presently, the military capabilities of the Palestinians have greatly diminished. Following the end of the Lebanese war in 1990, the main Palestinian armed presence was limited to the refugee camps. However, some groups have maintained an armed presence outside the camps.

The Lebanese Civil War

During the 1970s, Lebanon became a battleground for regional and international powers. The Palestinian presence in Lebanon played a key role in this as well as in sparking the war. The PLO's armed activities, both in South Lebanon and in Beirut, heightened tensions between them and Lebanese groups, specifically among the Christians. The Lebanese Civil War (1975-1990) was a complex and multifaceted conflict that had far-reaching consequences for Lebanon and the broader region. It was not a single war but rather a series of intertwined conflicts involving a variety of political, sectarian, and external conflicts. Other countries became involved either directly or through proxy groups. The war lasted for fifteen years and was devastating for Lebanon, reshaping its political and social landscape. By 1990, after much destruction and bloodshed, a peace accord, the Taif Agreement, was negotiated in Saudi Arabia and approved by the Lebanese government, bringing an end to the war. The agreement restructured the Lebanese political system, granting more power to Muslims, justified by the changing demographics, while keeping Christians in diminished key positions, though marginalized. After the war ended, Lebanon faced a long and difficult recovery process.

One of the legacies of the Civil War is Lebanon's enduring sectarian political system, which often paralyzes governance. The Taif Agreement sought to balance the interests of all religious groups, but it has entrenched the divide and is widely seen as a major obstacle to long-term stability and reform. Meanwhile, the country remains mired in political, economic, and social challenges. Despite the end of the Civil War, many of its root causes—sectarianism, external interference, and regional conflicts—remain unresolved. The legacy of the war, particularly in terms of divided political power and ongoing instability, continues to shape the country's trajectory.

The Syrian Occupation

Syria's official occupation of Lebanon is considered to be from 1990 to 2005 during the presidencies of Hafez al-Assad and his son Bashar al-Assad. In reality, this occurred much earlier. Hafez al-Assad intervened in the Lebanese Civil War by invading the country, in 1976, with more than 30,000 soldiers under the guise of keeping the peace and protecting the Christians. However, Syria's interests in Lebanon predate the 1976 intervention as Damascus had always raised a historical claim that considered Lebanon to be part of "Greater Syria." Lebanon, a much smaller country than Syria, gained its independence in 1943, and Syria gained its own independence in 1946, both from France. After this, the Syrian government was grudgingly content to keep what they referred to as "distinctive relations" with Lebanon, which gave Lebanon's stronger neighbor the pretense to interfere in the country's domestic and foreign politics. Thus, following the Taif Agreement, needlessly and unilaterally, Syria opted to maintain a significant military presence in Lebanon, exerting even more political influence and control over the country. This presence was widely resented and protested by many Lebanese, but it was not until after Bashar al-Assad was implicated in the assassination of Rafic Hariri, Lebanon's prime minister, in 2005, that massive protests led to pressuring Syria into withdrawing from Lebanon.

The Rise of Hezbollah

Hezbollah was founded in the early 1980s as a resistance movement, with widespread support among Lebanese Shia, who viewed it as defending Lebanese sovereignty, particularly against Israeli occupation in South Lebanon. After the Lebanese Civil War, as per the Taif Agreement, all armed groups outside the scope of official Lebanese Armed Forces were called to disarm. Hezbollah, which describes itself as a resistance group against Israeli occupation, was tacitly accepted by the government for exemption from disarming. This exemption was demanded by Syria, which had significant influence in Lebanon at the time. Syrian backing ensured that Hezbollah could continue to operate on its behalf, even if they were to reduce their own presence in Lebanon.

In reality, Syria supported Hezbollah as a Lebanese proxy to maximize its influence in Lebanon. Not only did Syria allow Hezbollah to retain its weapons, it even facilitated the transfer of arms and funds from Iran to Hezbollah. Iran, a Shia nation, was also seeking to develop its own sphere of influence in Lebanon and the region.

In 1992, Hezbollah decided to participate in elections and transitioned from being solely a militant group to a political party, gaining representation in parliament. This gave Hezbollah political legitimacy, which was leveraged to maintain an armed wing under the guise of resistance. Much as the Palestinians were able to do earlier, Hezbollah's military strength and political influence have allowed it to operate as a state within a state, with an infrastructure that mirrors Lebanon's, including military, banking, healthcare, social services, educational institutions, and more. As a political group, they provide social services, such as schools, hospitals, welfare programs, and financial services, bolstering their popularity and legitimacy. Iran's support of Hezbollah since its inception, both economically and logistically, has allowed it to maintain its military capabilities and expand its influence. In return, Iran views Hezbollah as a component of its broader regional strategy for influence in the Middle East.

The Lebanese state, divided along sectarian lines, has historically been reluctant and unable to enforce disarmament. Even calls to discuss conditions for disarmament have been met with resistance by Hezbollah, as the group has always argued that its weapons are necessary to defend Lebanon against external threats. This has led to a complex and continuing situation that has been detrimental for Lebanon and its citizens in many ways— politically, socially, and financially. More recently, in 2023-2024, a lengthy armed conflict between Hezbollah and Israel left large parts of the country, particularly in South Lebanon and Southern suburbs of Beirut, ravaged and destroyed, and the group's military capabilities severely degraded.

In September 2025, the Lebanese cabinet endorsed an army-led plan to maintain sole control on weapons within the state, effectively aiming to disarm Hezbollah. The plan is part of a broader ceasefire initiative with Israel resulting from the 2023-2024 war. However, no timeline was given, and Hezbollah strongly rejected the decision, calling it illegitimate and a threat to national sovereignty. The government also appealed for international financial support for reconstruction tied to the implementation of the disarmament plan.

Continued Instability and the Unending Waves of Emigration

Lebanon continued to face social, political, and security instability in the period after the Civil War and Syrian withdrawal, marked by frequent government deadlocks, corruption, and civil unrest. The country has struggled with economic crises that led to the collapse of the Lebanese currency and caused soaring unemployment and widespread poverty. The crisis of mismanagement and political corruption, compounded by the continued presence of domestic armed groups operating on behalf of regional regimes, has led to more violence as well as complete erosion of government oversight and the rule of law.

Lebanon's delicate sectarian balance, where different religious groups share political power, laid the foundation for some of this violence and turmoil. Over time, as demographics changed, specifically the growth of the Muslim population relative to Christians, this delicate balance has been disrupted, deepening tensions.

The political system seems increasingly outdated, the social situation is fragile, and the Lebanese political class remains out of touch with the needs of the population. Periodic protests demanding an overhaul of Lebanon's sectarian political system, accused of enabling corruption and impeding necessary reforms, give the country some moments of hope, but the path to stability and peace remains elusive. The election of a new president, Joseph Aoun, in 2025 and the subsequent formation of a new cabinet give hope, but it is too early to forecast whether they will succeed in putting Lebanon on the road to peace and prosperity.

The emigration of Lebanese from their homeland, which began early during the Arab conquests and peaked during the last of the Caliphates, the Ottoman Caliphate, has always been caused by two main factors: a quest for religious freedom and the desire for economic security. This emigration has continued through the present, although at varying intensity, for the very same reasons. However, seeking safety, security, and political stability have also become significant factors in the most recent times. While Lebanon is synonymous with historic emigration patterns triggered by religious persecution, economic hardships, political instability, and regional conflicts, the 1975-1990 Civil War and its aftermath significantly accelerated the outward movement of Lebanese to all parts of the world for all of these reasons combined. Families and individuals sought refuge in neighboring countries as well as faraway places. The war was characterized by horrific massacres and constant insecurity as well as the destruction of infrastructure, businesses, and livelihoods that pushed many Lebanese abroad. The period of the Civil War also created massive internal displacement. As the war intensified, many Lebanese, particularly those from urban centers experiencing active fighting like in Beirut, fled the violence to safer areas within Lebanon. Others were displaced for sectarian reasons.

After the end of the war and in the early 1990s, Lebanon faced significant challenges in rebuilding its economy and infrastructure. However, and more seriously, sectarian tensions continued, and the political system remained unstable, driving many more Lebanese to leave the country. While Lebanon experienced some post-war recovery lasting into the early 2000s, it was still caught in a cycle of instability causing political, economic, and security challenges. The continued presence of Syrian forces, the persistent presence of armed Lebanese factions, and the Israeli occupation in South Lebanon, as well as the constant threat of military actions, created an environment of uncertainty. Finally, as with the short-lived 2006 Israel-Hezbollah war, the much longer 2023-2024 war resulted in widespread devastation, especially in South Lebanon and parts of Beirut. The aftermath of such wars in the past deepened Lebanon's economic crisis and reinforced the desire for Lebanese to emigrate, and the recent wars have not been any different.

In the background of this prolonged period of instability and turmoil in Lebanon, the Syrian Civil War, which began in 2011 and ended in 2024, also had significant effects on Lebanon, particularly in terms of refugee flows. Lebanon hosted nearly two million Syrian refugees at the war's highest peak, putting immense strain on the country's resources, infrastructure, and economy. The spillover of the Syrian conflict aggravated the economic situation and increased insecurity in Lebanon.

Given all this violence, destruction, and loss of life over the past fifty years since the start of the Lebanese Civil War, it is not surprising that Lebanon's economy, which has faced serious challenges for years, has begun to deteriorate further. Political gridlock, corruption, and mismanagement of resources has led to mounting public discontent. Lebanon's financial system began to unravel in 2019, resulting in the Lebanese currency losing over 90 percent of its value against the U.S. dollar, leading to skyrocketing inflation and soaring unemployment. This economic collapse led to a new wave of emigration, as many young Lebanese, especially those with higher education, sought opportunities abroad to escape the dire economic conditions.

The major explosion at the Port of Beirut in August 2020 further eroded confidence in Lebanon's government and accelerated the decision for many to leave. Tragically, this explosion killed over two hundred people and injured more than six thousand, led to the displacement of more than three hundred thousand people, and caused widespread destruction to a large part of the city, devastating residential and business quarters. The explosion underscored the failure of the Lebanese state to ensure basic safety and governance.

As with earlier waves of migration, the Lebanese continued to move to the US, Canada, Europe, and Australia. However, one of the most common destinations now is the Gulf region. The Gulf states offer growing labor markets and a wide range of jobs, from skilled labor and administrative positions to technical and medical opportunities. The Lebanese have long had a presence in the Gulf and have always been welcomed and appreciated for their skills and expertise, but the war pushed a larger portion of the population there, especially since the Gulf is close to Lebanon and shares many cultural traits with Lebanon.

There is a bright side in the midst of these new waves of emigration, as was the case with earlier ones, and that is the lifelines they provide for many individuals and families in Lebanon that secure their sustenance and other needs from remittances sent by members of the Lebanese diaspora abroad. The trend of Lebanese emigrating in search of peace and prosperity, even though it is marked by several waves and influenced by unfolding situations, has essentially been continuous and seems unending.

Despite this turbulent history, in the end, Lebanon remained the only part of the Eastern Mediterranean region where the majority of the population did not convert to Islam. In Lebanon, Christianity thrived. Those who were compelled to migrate out of Lebanon remained loyal to their country and faith. Saint Maron, who left the riches of the world behind in Antioch to live as a hermit on top of a hill to devote himself to prayers and contemplation, had his statue placed on the outer wall of Saint Peter's Basilica in the Vatican in 2011 by Pope Benedict XVI. Communal organization and the ability to adapt ensured the survival and continuity of Lebanon's Christian communities. Let this be a lesson for the Christians at home and abroad.

Saint Maron's statue on the outer wall of Saint Peter's Basilica, unveiled in 2011 by Pope Benedict XVI

However, attention must now turn to Lebanon's future—for all of its citizens, both within the country and abroad—and, more importantly, to the role Christians of Lebanon should play in ensuring their continued presence in a renewed national identity. This role should reflect the historic contributions they made in shaping Lebanon as a homeland not only for themselves, but also for others who now share it with them. As someone shaped by this legacy, I feel a deep sense of responsibility and hope for what we, together in faith, can still build.

AFTERWORD:

A Roadmap for Sustained Growth and Development for Lebanon

WHILE THE LEBANESE PEOPLE CAN trace their ethnic and religious roots back in so many different directions, including to ancient Lebanon itself, today they share a common future. That future, while not apparent at the present time, nevertheless exists. Lebanon is a place where pluralism has been a defining characteristic of its history, culture, and society for millennia. Its population is a living testament to the multiple civilizations that have called this land home. Our Phoenician ancestors established one of the first global trade routes, and their alphabet became the precursor to many writing systems still in use today. From the Greeks to the Romans and Byzantines, and from the Arabs to the French, each has left a lasting imprint on Lebanon's cultural, religious, and social fabric. This layered history—a powerful reminder of how the past has shaped the present—remains deeply woven into the national identity of Lebanon. Each of these civilizations helped lay the groundwork for what has become the modern Lebanese identity.

Lebanon's complex web of ethnicities, religions, and cultures has been both a source of strength and a point of contention.

Despite the sectarian divisions that have defined the country's past, the Lebanese people share a goal that transcends their differences and unites them in their desire to rebuild their nation. Byzantium and Antioch enriched the faith traditions of the Orthodox, Melkite, and Maronite Christians. Arabia brought with it a new culture, religion, and language. Sunni, Shia, and Druze Muslims each have contributed to the richness of Lebanon's religious mosaic, unified by Arabic as the official language. Together, these communities have found a lasting home in the historic Land of Canaan.

This complex society has yielded an equally complex political arrangement since Lebanon's post-independence era—an intricate system of sectarian power-sharing that reflects the country's religious divisions. The goal of this sectarian system—in which an identity of faith is defined by emphasis on doctrine and creedal statements—was to prevent any single sect from dominating others, guaranteeing that each community had a voice in national governance. This arrangement was later enshrined in the Taif Agreement of 1989, which formally ended the Lebanese Civil War and restructured Lebanon's political system, ostensibly in an effort to preserve peace and stability. Though the agreement was hastily superimposed onto the existing National Pact, its intention was to ensure representation for each of Lebanon's major religious sects and prevent any one group from monopolizing political power.

However, while designed to maintain peace and facilitate postwar recovery, the system has produced several unintended negative consequences. Over time, it has further reinforced sectarian identities, sometimes at the expense of a unified national identity. It has also contributed to political gridlock, fostered corruption, and abetted the perpetuation of a deep state network that continues to undermine reform and frustrate public trust. These persistent challenges have led many Lebanese citizens to question the utility of this system, and I am one of those people.

To be clear: Lebanon's current political structure is ineffective and cannot sustain the growth and development necessary for the country to be a viable nation.

The Shared Future of Lebanon: A Nation of Pluralism and Unity

The most significant challenge facing Lebanon today is the balance of legitimate sectarian identities with the need to create a contemporary, inclusive, and unified state. Many Lebanese have already called for reforms to reduce the role of religion in politics and governance, advocating instead for a secular, transparent, efficient, and more accountable government. While it may have been a necessity for peace in the aftermath of the Civil War (1975-1990), the current sectarian system remains a legacy that continues to affect Lebanon's political and economic viability, contributing to corruption, financial mismanagement, and weakened governance.

Lebanon would benefit from a reclaimed national identity defined not by religion but by a shared commitment to the country's future peace and prosperity. Such an identity inherently prioritizes the common good over sectarian interests and offers a unique opportunity for unity among Lebanon's diverse citizens. Lebanon's diaspora, now integrated into the homeland more than ever, can also play a significant role in shaping the country's future. With millions of Lebanese expatriates worldwide, Lebanon benefits from a powerful network of accomplished individuals and groups maintaining strong ties to their homeland. Historically, the diaspora has played a pivotal role in advocating for Lebanon, especially during times of crisis. Their influence extends beyond economics to include cultural and political spheres. Many Lebanese abroad have become advocates for reform and proponents of a non-sectarian, progressive Lebanon, pushing for a stronger national identity, modern governance, and mechanisms of accountability. This connection underscores that Lebanon's future is not limited to its borders but is part of a broader global Lebanese identity that transcends religious and sectarian divisions. As the history I have presented in this book documents, this global identity is congruent with the history of the Levant.

The Need for Secularism in Lebanon's Governance

My position on religion, and my Christian belief, has been evident throughout this book. However, I strongly believe in the separation of church and state. Creating a governance system in Lebanon that is free from religious interference would constitute a radical departure from the country's current political structure. A secular governance system would transcend religious identities, assigning responsibilities and authority based on the principle of equality for all citizens, regardless of their religion. This shift would dismantle the sectarian power-sharing model and replace it with a structure that promotes meritorious leadership, fair representation, and genuine national unity. Three key characteristics must be met in order to successfully implement such a secular governance system in Lebanon: the separation of religion and state, a democratic electoral process with inclusive representation, and the establishment of independent government institutions.

In a fully secular Lebanon, there would be a clear separation between religion and the state. Religious laws would no longer influence the country's civil code or political processes. Laws governing marriage, divorce, inheritance, and personal status—long governed by sectarian traditions inherited from the Ottoman era—would instead be regulated by universal civil laws that apply to all Lebanese citizens equally. Religious institutions would not hold political power or exert direct influence over the state, and government positions would no longer be allocated based on sectarian affiliation. Political parties and candidates would compete based on ideology, policy, and merit, rather than religious identity.

In a secular Lebanon, the electoral system would move toward a more democratic and inclusive model. Representation would be based on citizenship rather than religious affiliation. Instead of electing according to sectarian identity, candidates would be selected for their political views, experience, and ability to serve the national interest. A proportional representation system—which allows for a more balanced distribution of power—would provide broader representation for diverse political ideologies and social groups, giving all Lebanese citizens a voice, regardless of their sect or religion. In local elections, secular political parties and civil society groups would likely rise in prominence, challenging traditional sectarian and familial politics.

Furthermore, in a secular Lebanon, the executive, legislative, and judicial branches of government would function independently of religious institutions. The positions of president, prime minister, and speaker of parliament would no longer be assigned based on religion. This secularity is the most difficult of the requisite characteristics to implement, given the entrenched nature of the current political system and the perceived sense of security it conveys to different religious sects through guaranteed representation. However, instituting meritocratic principles for selecting individuals to serve in these important positions—such as executive ability, honesty, integrity, professional competence, and vision for the future—offers a more rational and equitable approach than sectarian allocation.

Parliament would ideally include both independent and party-affiliated representatives, including members from secular parties, women's groups, and civil society organizations, all of whom advocate for policies that benefit the broader population rather than specific sectarian interests. The judiciary would function as an impartial and ethical institution, applying laws based on constitutional principles rather than religious rulings or political interference. This would ensure fair justice to all citizens, regardless of a person's religion.

Similarly, a secular Lebanon would ideally have a government that is inclusive, transparent, and accountable to all of its citizens, regardless of their religion. Naturally, given the nuances of Lebanese society, reforms would be implemented gradually, guided by consultation, consensus building, and inclusivity. Assurances for guaranteeing religious freedom, respecting civil rights, and revitalizing the economy are necessary for obtaining cross-societal and generational support for such a massive change.

While Lebanon's current sectarian system grants each sect political power, a secular system would not. However, a secular system must guarantee freedom of religion while ensuring that no religious group holds political power or influence over state functions. All Lebanese citizens, regardless of their religious affiliation, would be guaranteed the right to worship freely without state interference. At the same time, individual religious beliefs would not dictate one's public or political role. There would be no requirement for citizens to register their religion or identify with a sect in official documents or political participation.

A secular Lebanon would be expected to promote equality across all sectors of society—ethnicity, gender, and socioeconomic status—including in government, education, and employment. Under the current political system, women remain significantly underrepresented in political offices. Secularism, however, can pave the way for greater representation for women and minority groups, protect the rights of children against violence and exploitation, and uphold human rights principles that provide equal legal protection for all citizens.

A policy of economic revitalization—one that prioritizes national development, expands employment opportunities, and ensures social welfare rather than serving sectarian interests—would be needed given the dire financial situation facing a large segment of the Lebanese population. Resource allocation must be based on need, not sectarian affiliation. Government funding and public resources should be distributed to where the need is obvious and documented, particularly in the most underdeveloped regions and marginalized sectors of society. Lebanon's private sector can thrive without the constraints of sectarian networks. New investments, both domestic and global, would be attracted, positioning Lebanon as a more competitive player on the international stage. Secular governance would encourage a more transparent economic system, where anti-corruption reforms would be enacted, without resistance, to ensure accountability and responsibility.

A Technocratic Model for Lebanon

I believe advocating for a technocratic form of governance in Lebanon best reflects the urgent need for serious political and economic reform, especially considering the country's long-standing struggle with corruption, sectarianism, and mismanagement. Such a framework would offer the country a path to greater stability, accountability, and efficiency—especially critical during the initial period should Lebanon transition into a secular society. However, the success of such a system would depend on instituting sincere and genuine reforms. Lebanon does not lack talent or creativity; rather, it simply lacks a functioning structure to effectively harness these strengths. I have identified twelve pillars that, collectively, offer a robust and viable technocratic model of governance upon which a new Lebanon can be rebuilt.

Technocratic Orientation – Separating Politics from Policy

Put more specifically, what would a technocratic orientation look like in Lebanon—one in which executive leaders of Lebanon working at the highest levels of the government, particularly Cabinet members, are selected for their experience in their professional fields rather than for political or sectarian affiliation? Parliament could then take on the role of strengthening democracy by stimulating well-informed public discussions for forming broad consensus regarding institutional changes to be pursued in support of reforms. The president, as head of state and symbol of national unity, would continue to uphold and defend the constitution, ensuring adherence to the rule of law. There is practical precedence for this model in many established democracies.

However, Lebanon faces key structural limitations in adopting a fully technocratic Cabinet. Although the Constitution allows the prime minister to nominate Cabinet officers, they must be confirmed or rejected by the Parliament through a vote of confidence. Furthermore, Cabinet officers may simultaneously hold seats in the Parliament and are not required to resign their legislative posts upon appointment to the executive branch. In Lebanon, career politicians have long been unduly influenced by political, social, and religious ideologies—factors which have led to fragmentation and stagnation. Therefore, this is a good place to start a change that paves the way for technocrats and academicians to be sought, as a norm, for Cabinet membership as experts in their field of study or practice, who can achieve policy reform and economic restructuring. To ensure accountability, the parliamentary system of Lebanon—similar to that of many other industrialized nations—could continue to have Cabinet approval rights through the vote of confidence mechanism.

A Federated System of Governance – Overcoming the Challenge of Centralization and Religious Division

In many post-conflict nations, the struggle to balance the interests of multiple factions—religious, ethnic, or regional—often becomes a significant barrier to national unity and progress. This is the current situation in Lebanon. A highly centralized government exacerbates struggle by creating a top-down structure that does not account for the diversity of local needs or aspirations. The government, in such systems, tends to become more of a bottleneck than a catalyst for improvement. Inefficiency at every level of government often makes it difficult for citizens to feel any positive impact from government services, which may lead to deepened feelings of frustration, alienation, and division among different groups. Compounding this issue is the lack of local autonomy regarding minor administrative matters. Such a governance structure is incapable of allowing communities to make decisions that directly impact their lives, creating resentment and disempowerment.

A federated system is one in which power is shared between a central government and various smaller regional governments or local entities, each of which is granted a significant degree of autonomy. This opportunity-structure model allows for local decision-making and governance—that is, people from different regions or cultures can make decisions that are tailored to their own specific needs and values, rather than being forced to conform to a one-size-fits-all policy imposed by a distant, centralized authority.

A decentralized governance can help reduce social and political tension in a number of ways. For example, in a decentralized federation, different regions or local entities could engage in healthy competition, striving to improve the welfare of their citizens. This competition can manifest in improving education, healthcare, infrastructure, or economic opportunities. Since local governments have more control over their budgets and policies, they would likely seek the most efficient and effective solutions to meet the needs of their people. This process encourages innovation and the sharing of best practices between regions, leading to overall national progress. Decentralization also increases accountability because local leaders will be directly responsible to the people they serve, and citizens have the ability to demand change or even elect new leadership—thus creating a greater sense of democratic participation and reducing feelings of powerlessness, which often fuel dissatisfaction and division.

While decentralization offers clear advantages, it is not a panacea. A federated system requires that different local regions find ways to collaborate and build unity despite their differences. Since divisions may remain a challenge even in a decentralized system, it is important to ensure that the framework encourages inter-regional cooperation and national identity while respecting local autonomy. For this system to succeed, it is essential that people see themselves not just as members of their specific group, but as part of a larger national community. It is through such local empowerment and national cooperation that long-lasting social stability and progress could be achieved.

Credible Public Education – The Bedrock of Democracy

A strong educational system provides individuals the knowledge and skills necessary to engage in society effectively, make informed decisions, and contribute to economic and social progress. A skilled workforce—essential for innovation and productivity—is cultivated through quality education that prepares citizens for the demands of modern industries. In a broader sense, education shapes a society's values, culture, and social cohesion, enabling citizens to navigate complex issues, participate in democratic processes, and create a more prosperous, equitable future.

For Lebanon, rebuilding its education system would be key to breaking the cycle of high unemployment, economic collapse, and societal instability. While Lebanon maintains stringent national education standards and oversight, outdated curricula and significant disparities exist between the public and private sectors, primarily due to chronic underfunding of public education. Simply put, Lebanon lacks the necessary investment to improve its public educational environment. The issue, however, goes beyond questions of funding and oversight—or whether control is localized or centralized. Both models have demonstrated merit, with successful examples found around the world. The more urgent concern is whether education is tune with industrial needs, economic realities, and aspirations of the Lebanese people. By all accounts, the current educational system is not.

To address this disconnect, the education system must be reformed to prioritize digital skills—including coding, artificial Intelligence literacy, and technical training—in addition to critical thinking, problem-solving skills, and scientific inquiry. Also, a key aspect of any reform is to place emphasis on universal values into the curriculum.

This would encourage Lebanon's youth to think beyond sectarian identities and embrace a unified national ethos.

When public education becomes a priority, appropriately funded and delivered, it allows students from all sects and backgrounds to learn together in an environment of mutual respect and equality. A robust education system at all levels—enhanced by a strong technological orientation, an entrepreneurial mindset, and a multilingual talent base—would be a formidable combination for an emerging, but lagging, knowledge economy of Lebanon. Such a potential would also create opportunities and incentives for Lebanon's youth to remain and thrive in their homeland, helping to reverse the country's persistent brain drain.

Energy Security – A Fundamental Requirement

Lebanon's path to economic recovery and attracting foreign investments hinges on the urgent need to rebuild its energy infrastructure destroyed during the long period of war. Specifically, the country's power sector is now dominated by an inefficient state-run company and a chaotic network of privately owned power generators. This is supported by an outdated grid and heavy reliance on imported fossil fuels—factors that expose Lebanon to global price fluctuations and supply disruptions, making electricity even less reliable and costly. This chronic energy insecurity has severely hampered economic growth.

Lebanon's energy crisis has created a vicious cycle: high generator costs unfairly burden households, discourage local business expansion, and deter foreign investors wary of a lack of stable operational environments. Without reliable power, even the most promising sectors for Lebanon, such as tourism, cannot thrive. For energy-intensive sectors such as manufacturing and high-tech, the current conditions are practically unworkable.

To break this cycle, Lebanon must prioritize energy reforms. This starts by investing in decentralized renewable energy solutions, like solar and wind, that are both sustainable and cost-effective, as well as promoting public-private partnerships and implementing transparent governance. Solar and wind energy offer a promising solution to allow the country to reduce dependency on fuel imports, stabilize energy prices, and enhance grid reliability. Most importantly, more reliance on alternative energy sources would help Lebanon reduce its environmental impact. Until the power sector is stabilized and modernized, Lebanon will struggle to rebuild investor confidence and reverse its economic decline—and therefore will be unable to resolve its chronic unemployment situation.

Digital Readiness – Key to Innovation

Governments have an important role to play in markets, and the digital world is no exception. Digital readiness offers an opportunity to developing countries to narrow their gap with developed economies. Information and computing technologies—their tools and services, models and impact—can provide a vehicle for growth. As the global economy was rapidly digitizing, Lebanon was falling further behind. This will continue unless the country takes decisive steps to rebuild its digital capabilities and restore its competitiveness. Lebanon must now invest in modernizing its digital infrastructure by expanding broadband access, deploying fiber-optic networks, and attracting investment in emerging technologies. These initiatives must be implemented across the entire country—not just in Beirut and other major cities—to ensure equitable economic development.

Digital transformation must also extend to governance. Streamlining public services, enhancing transparency, and implementing cybersecurity protections are essential to attracting foreign investment and restoring public trust. While there is a very significant cost for doing all this, the costs of inaction are far greater. Failing to invest will exacerbate Lebanon's already existing digital inequities and limit its ability to participate in the modern global economy. However, by itself, technology will not provide solutions; rather, technology must be at the center of a broad family of public policies that address a wide range of issues, including policy strategies to exploit technology's capabilities in order to achieve economic value.

Critical Infrastructure – Path to Economic Recovery

Lebanon's once-advanced infrastructure made it a recognized hub for trade, commerce, and culture in the Middle East. To reclaim its former prominence and enable sustainable economic recovery, Lebanon must reinvest in its critical infrastructure, expand its capacity, and develop innovative services that can compete with the rapidly developing nations in the region. This would require revitalizing key sectors such as aviation, maritime ports, railways, and urban transit systems.

Lebanon's only international airport in Beirut is an aging infrastructure with insufficient capacity to handle growing demand. A significant upgrade is essential—not only to expand terminal capacity, modernize facilities, and improve service quality, but also to position Lebanon as a regional transit point for both business and tourism. Moreover, Lebanon cannot support these industries with a single civil airport; additional regional airports must be considered to ensure long-term accessibility and resilience to a growing economy.

Lebanon's maritime infrastructure, particularly the Port of Beirut, has historically been one of the most important trade gateways in the Mediterranean. Yet, the 2020 explosion that severely damaged the port compounded existing challenges such as outdated facilities and limited capacity. Rebuilding and modernizing this port—and expanding operational capabilities of other ports, such as those in Tripoli and Sidon—should be urgent national priorities.

Lebanon once operated a sophisticated railway system until the start of the 1975 Civil War, connecting its major cities and other regional points. However, years of neglect have left the network totally dysfunctional. Reviving and modernizing this railway system must also be a top priority. A comprehensive rail network that serves not only urban centers but also rural and remote areas would offer a sustainable, efficient, and cost-effective transportation alternative. Moreover, integrating Lebanon's rail network with regional rail systems would further increase its role as a transit hub between Europe, the Arab world, and Asia. Additionally, reviving the train system would alleviate traffic congestion, reduce environmental pollution, and create jobs—making it an essential part of the country's long-term recovery plan.

Beirut, like many major cities, is plagued by chronic traffic congestion, causing delays, lost productivity, and environmental degradation. A modern subway system that connects the city center with its rapidly expanding suburbs would alleviate these issues by providing efficient, sustainable urban transport to thousands of residents. A well-designed subway system would not only enhance urban mobility but also contribute to environmental sustainability by reducing the reliance on private vehicles. Additionally, with population growth and suburban development, it is critical that any new public transport system be integrated with future urban planning to ensure long-term success.

The most realistic approach for financing Lebanon's critical infrastructure projects is to leverage public-private partnerships. Collaborating with international companies that offer both technical expertise and financial resources would reduce the fiscal burden on the government while ensuring that projects are completed efficiently and with high standards. In parallel, Lebanon must expand its investment in critical services outside Beirut and its metropolitan area—including higher education, transportation, public safety, healthcare, water, and sanitation—to ensure a balanced approach to development.

Administrative Modernization – Maximizing Foreign Investment

The expansion of foreign investment could significantly improve Lebanon's financial outlook and employment rate. However, the country is not adequately prepared to attract and sustain foreign investment. Its bureaucratic system is too rigid and cumbersome, limiting its ability to respond to emerging economic opportunities. Successfully attracting foreign corporations would expand the volume of administrative and legal transactions in the country. To operate profitably, these companies would require access to efficient professional services—delivered without unnecessary obstacles.

As of now, the inefficient bureaucratic labor system is a hindrance to promoting a modern, competitive economy. This makes it essential to review and restructure existing policies to align with changing industry and business models. To maximize foreign investment, Lebanon must ensure a stable and transparent regulatory environment by committing to clear legal frameworks and empowering independent oversight bodies. Streamlining investment processes and reducing bureaucratic burdens are critical steps toward making market entry attractive.

In addition to market entry, Lebanon must also prioritize investor retention. This includes offering long-term incentives such as tax credits, infrastructure support, and co-investment opportunities in strategic sectors—for example, renewable energy. Dedicated agencies should be established to support investors for business expansion, assist with regulatory compliance, and facilitate reinvestment.

Credible integration into international trade networks through bilateral investment treaties, free trade agreements, and digital trade frameworks would project Lebanon as a reliable and forward-looking investment partner. Finally, these efforts must be backed by strong anti-corruption measures, including efficient dispute resolution mechanisms. A credible and impartial judicial system is essential to reinforcing this foundation by protecting investor rights and the enforcement of contracts.

Sustainable Development – Integrated Recovery

Lebanon is facing an environmental crisis resulting from years of neglect. From polluted coastlines and rivers to unmanaged waste and crumbling infrastructure—nearly every essential component of clean and healthy living has been compromised. Pollution and environmental degradation are widespread, and Lebanon has already wasted and destroyed vast amounts of natural resources, with water and forests at the top of the list.

The relationship between economic growth and environmental quality is complex. While rapid technological progress and industrialization can indeed have negative implications on environmental capacity in terms of energy needs, sustainable development remains achievable. Economic, ecological, and social priorities do not have to be in conflict. However, they require well-designed governmental policies addressing the potential environmental impacts alongside market growth in parallel to industrialization. Environmental sustainability must therefore be integral to Lebanon's recovery and development agenda.

As Lebanon plans its economic recovery and national rebuilding, it must be done in harmony with environmental protection—or risk deepening the country's ecological decline. A strong environmental governance framework is urgently needed: one that can enforce standards, oversee development projects, and ensure that sustainability is a non-negotiable pillar of national planning.

Top priority must also be given to waste and wastewater management. Irresponsible waste disposal and untreated sewage have already led to widespread health and ecological consequences. Investments in decentralized waste systems, wastewater treatment plants, and recycling infrastructure are essential to stop further environmental and social damage. Such an agenda would also create new green jobs and stimulate sustainable economic activity.

Natural ecosystems, long degraded by illegal construction, quarrying, and wildfires, must be protected and restored. Reforestation programs and the rehabilitation of rivers and coastlines are crucial steps toward environmental resilience. Urban planning must also be reimagined to prioritize green spaces, climate-resistant infrastructure, and responsible zoning to prevent further urban sprawl.

A truly sustainable recovery requires community engagement, education, and support for local environmental initiatives. In fact, every entity in Lebanon has a role to play in restoring the country's natural balance. Environmental reform is not optional—it is the foundation for any meaningful and lasting recovery. For Lebanon to create a dignified, livable, and resilient future, it must begin by healing the land it stands on. It is a necessity for long-term economic stability, public health, and national dignity—all while improving quality of life.

Innovation and Competition – Positioning Lebanon

While Lebanon has significant human capital, it lacks the institutional and material resources to turn its innovative potential into tangible economic growth. This commitment to innovation is necessary to make Lebanon an appealing destination for international businesses seeking a strategic foothold in the region. While offering the necessary infrastructures is a foundational step, Lebanon must also distinguish itself by supporting truly unique or disruptive initiatives. Establishing an institutional framework that supports niche entrepreneurial initiatives would enable it to carve out a distinctive position in the regional and global market.

Lebanon must support a credible startup culture by adopting targeted measures such as tax incentives, technology hubs, and access to local and global mentorship networks. Engaging the country's highly skilled diaspora is equally essential—by encouraging investment and promoting knowledge transfer, Lebanon can benefit from the expertise and capital of its citizens. A peaceful Lebanon would also be well-positioned to attract investment capital from its own neighboring nations who have always been supportive of Lebanon and appreciative of the talents within.

Free economic zones offer a promising tool to stimulate domestic industry and reduce the emigration of the trained workforce out of the country. Among additional measures, reducing the corporate tax rate can help stimulate economic investments. However, corporate tax reform does not mean an aggregate tax cut for the overall economy. Any potential loss in government revenue can be balanced by increasing collection in all sectors of the economy—from personal income to corporate earnings—through enforcement and automation.

Currently, Lebanon operates a limited number of free economic zones, primarily administered through the Port of Beirut. Expanding and optimizing these zones must become a key pillar of the reformed economy. Many more of these initiatives are needed to draw in significant corporate presence. However, there is a risk that corporations will invest only for as long as there are favorable conditions for making large profits. Therefore, it is critical to establish a policy framework that creates incentives for long-term capital investment in key economic sectors.

Universities can also play a role in strengthening Lebanon's economic outlook in the local and competitive global markets. Given the concentrated human intellectual capital on their campuses, universities are better equipped to provide guidance, expertise, and resources that individual entrepreneurs and small businesses need to scale. This kind of investment will bring important returns to universities by making internships and hands-on opportunities available to their students to better prepare them for the job market. There are already examples of university-based technology centers dedicated to incubation and innovation. However, to achieve meaningful national impact, such initiatives must become ubiquitous.

Cultural Reinvestment – Capitalizing on the Multilingual Workforce

Lebanon is historically synonymous with its polyglot society. Its recovery will need to extend beyond rebuilding physical and digital infrastructure; it must also invest in human capital, particularly in language and cultural education. In a country characterized by multilingual and multicultural influences, the core languages—Arabic, French, and English—and sometimes other languages, such as Armenian, depending on their community—have produced world citizens.

While citizens of Lebanon often fiercely adhere to the communities that represent them, educational settings often transcend such divisions. Through empathy, communication, collaboration, critical thinking, awareness, and exposure to diverse perspectives—alongside employment resulting from developed skills—learners become cosmopolitan in thought and action. Language acquisition and mastery are central to this development, enabling broader understanding and deeper engagement across cultures.

As the global economy demands foreign language proficiency, Lebanon's polyglot society holds a unique competitive advantage. This linguistic diversity significantly contributes to the country's economic recovery, regional influence, and global standing. Lebanon must build on this strong asset by putting in place programs at schools and local communities that provide language proficiency to anyone who seeks it.

Beyond just being a linguistic trait, the ability to speak multiple languages allows for greater flexibility in trade, cultural exchange, and diplomacy. Capitalizing on this linguistic diversity, Lebanon can further strengthen its position in bridging divides and enhancing its societal and cultural influence.

Health and Human Services – Social Stratification

For decades, Lebanon was classified by the World Bank as an upper-middle-income country, marked by relative economic stability and a high standard of living. However, a prolonged period of instability and a devastating economic crisis—coupled with a sharp depreciation of its currency—have since pushed Lebanon into a lower-middle-income status. The repercussions of this crisis have been catastrophic for the Lebanese people, undermining their ability to meet even basic needs, let alone afford education or healthcare.

As the country struggles under the weight of poverty, inflation, and unemployment, the Lebanese government and supportive nations, alongside international organizations, must take swift action to mitigate the crisis while laying the groundwork for a more sustainable future. The first priority must be currency stabilization. Although a full recovery of the Lebanese pound may not be feasible, the government must explore exchange-rate management tools to curb volatility and accelerate negotiations with the international community to secure urgently needed financial assistance.

The credibility of Lebanon's banking sector—once a pillar of its economy—has been severely damaged due to restrictions on withdrawals and lack of transparency. Comprehensive banking reform is critical to restoring confidence. These reforms should focus on improving the transparency and functionality of the sector, while implementing controls in a managed and equitable way to prevent further erosion and ensure access to personal savings for Lebanese citizens.

The crushing impact of Lebanon's economic collapse is most acutely felt by its most vulnerable populations. To alleviate this, the government must implement social safety nets, focusing on immediate needs such as food, healthcare, and education, providing families with the financial cushion to survive the worst effects of inflation. Specifically, access to education has become increasingly difficult for Lebanese citizens. The high cost of living and devaluation of the currency have made these basic services inaccessible for many. To address this imbalance, the government must increase funding for public education and subsidize private education to make schooling affordable for all.

In parallel, the government must urgently address Lebanon's healthcare crisis. Many hospitals operate with limited resources and lack essential medicines, while public health infrastructure remains under severe strain. The government must work with international health agencies to secure discounted pharmaceuticals and provide essential medical supplies to hospitals. Additionally, subsidized health insurance programs should be introduced to cover those who are unable to afford treatment.

Lebanon's mental health crisis—exacerbated by the financial collapse—also requires immediate attention. Widespread stress, anxiety, and depression must be met with accessible, well-resourced mental health services integrated into the healthcare response system.

Rebuilding Social Norms – A New Post-Conflict Society for Lebanon

Despite having lived as an expatriate in the United States for over four decades, I remained connected to my birthplace—a country that I lived in for the first two decades of my life. My routine visits have increasingly revealed the profound scars left by half a century of internal and regional conflicts, resulting in extensive physical and psychological damage. While significant efforts are required for rebuilding the infrastructure, it is equally important to address the collapse of prevailing norms at every level of society. From interpersonal interactions to transportation, the fabric that once held the society together seems to have unraveled. It is clear to me that restoring the human element that governs daily life is essential for true recovery and long-term stability.

The most shocking part of my observations is that people no longer seem to recognize the breakdown of social systems, let alone discuss it. The gradual erosion of these norms has become so ingrained that basic behaviors, like how to communicate respectfully, cooperate with others, or even navigate the roads, have all but disappeared. These behaviors may seem trivial, but they are the backbone of any functional society. Without these norms, societies begin to fragment, becoming less cohesive and more mistrustful. When such a collapse occurs, the damage may be invisible at first but its effect is immediate, from the very ways people relate to one another to how they relate to local and national governments. In times of prolonged conflict, survival becomes the primary concern, and norms that ensure mutual respect and cooperation are relegated to secondary importance.

Physical infrastructure may be rebuilt with sound planning and adequate resources, but the human element—the social cohesion that allows people to live and work together in peace—requires a much deeper, more intentional effort. A purposeful program to rebuild these social norms across all segments and levels of society is urgently needed. However, restoring social norms cannot be a top-down initiative driven by the government alone. A collaborative effort between government institutions and grassroots movements would be the most effective approach. Each has unique strengths that, when combined, can offer a comprehensive solution to rebuilding the human aspect of the nation. The government plays a crucial role in providing the resources, policy support, and coordination needed to scale any initiative. It can ensure the program is available nationwide, integrating it into the education system and public services. The government's backing lends the program legitimacy, encouraging widespread participation. Public campaigns, through mass media, could further amplify the program's reach. Grassroots movements are equally vital. They are rooted in the local context and are often more trusted by community members than national institutions, which gives them the ability to adapt programs to local needs and ensure that they resonate with the people they aim to help. Furthermore, grassroots movements are better positioned to foster a sense of ownership and community among participants. They can model behaviors in real-life contexts, leading by example, and organizing local events that encourage people to engage with one another constructively. Together, the government and grassroots movements can ensure both reach and depth. Such a program must also assume continued instability and be adaptable to shifting conditions, particularly in uncertain times.

The success of such an initiative would depend not only on its ability to launch but also on its capacity to sustain itself over time. The ongoing instability in the country means that any initiative must be self-sustaining and capable of evolving. One key strategy is to build community-led networks that can continue the work independently. Once the program has begun, local leaders would be trained to lead workshops and facilitate discussions, reducing the dependency on external actors. The work of restoring social norms will not be easy or quick, especially in a context of continued instability. But by focusing on human resilience the social cohesion necessary for long-term peace and stability could be rebuilt. It is through this collective effort that a fractured society can begin to heal—not only physically but also spiritually.

Challenges of Transitioning to a Secular System

Transitioning from Lebanon's current sectarian system to a secular one will undoubtedly face several challenges, including overcoming sectarianism in society, averting political resistance, and effecting constitutional and legal reforms.

Lebanon's deep-rooted sectarian identities cannot be changed overnight. Many Lebanese people have been raised with sectarian loyalties, and religious leaders continue to hold significant influence over public opinion. Therefore, transitioning to secular governance will require a cultural shift toward national unity and social cohesion.

Lebanese politicians and political parties who benefit from the current system will likely resist secular reforms. They have established their power bases through sectarian channels. Dismantling this system would significantly diminish their influence. Therefore, any transition to secularism will require political focus, widespread public support, and the ability to overcome the vested interests that maintain the status quo.

The current Lebanese Constitution is heavily influenced by sectarian quotas and power-sharing arrangements. In order to transition to secular governance, the Constitution would need to be revised to eliminate sectarian provisions, and new laws must be enacted to ensure equality and prevent discrimination. While these changes are neither easy nor straightforward, they are necessary to rebuild a functioning society.

The Future that Awaits

Lebanon stands at a crossroads. Its future, though shaped by centuries of ethnic and religious strife, offers an opportunity to redefine what it means to be Lebanese. As the country's younger generation rises to demand change, there is a growing hope that Lebanon can forge a new identity—one defined not by sect, but by shared values of unity, democracy, and freedom. Moving forward will require overcoming sectarian divisions and embracing a collective vision grounded in the common good.

Lebanon must continue to navigate the complexities of sectarian society while striving for the reforms that will allow it to grow beyond its broken system. A nation that honors its historical pluralism while embracing a shared future has the potential to become again a beacon of coexistence in the Middle East. While the transition to a secular governance system in Lebanon will undoubtedly be difficult, it offers a pathway toward a more inclusive, equal, and democratic society, marking the beginning of a new chapter, one where the Lebanese people are united not by their differences, but by a shared national identity.

Despite the complexities of its past and present, Lebanon remains a country of immense potential. Its pluralism—often seen as its fault lines—can become its greatest strength. The shared struggles of its people—whether in resisting occupation, surviving famine and disease, or enduring political dysfunction and economic collapse—form the common bonds that unite them. The journey toward secularism will demand compromise, dialogue, and sustained effort. Yet, the vision of a unified, prosperous Lebanon—free from the constraints of sectarianism—is a vision that many Lebanese citizens continue to believe in.

The challenges to our culture and identity, should we remain complacent, are formidable. The impact of current and potential regional conflicts remains substantial, threatening to further erode our national cohesion. A question often asked is: why do the Lebanese excel abroad more than they do in their home country? I would posit that, when expatriates excel, it is because of the values we learned in Lebanon regarding family, community, and hard work. We excel not despite being Lebanese, but because we are Lebanese.

The twelve pillars I have proposed here are offered in the hope that mothers no longer have to weep at airports as their sons and daughters leave in search of opportunity elsewhere. In our heterogeneity lies our salvation. We must learn to embrace our differences—not as divisions, but as sources of strength. This effort will require everyone's abilities, ideas, and aspirations.

Let us rise to the moment. Let us build a Lebanon worthy of its people.

WORKS CITED AND CONSULTED

Part One

Alouf, Michael M. 1999. *History of Baalbek*. American Press.

Beggiani, Seely. 2003. *Aspects of Maronite History*. Saint Maron Publications.

Bertman, Stephen. 2005. *Handbook to Life in Ancient Mesopotamia*. Oxford University Press.

Collelo, Thomas. 1987. *Lebanon: A Country Study*. Federal Research Division of the Library of Congress.

Cory, Isaac Preston. 1832. *Sacred Texts: Ancient Fragments. The Theology of the Phoenicians from Sanchoniatho*. Web.

Dib, Pierre. 1971. *History of the Maronite Church*. Translated by Seely Beggiani. Imprimerie Catholique.

Dumper, Michael R. T., and Bruce E. Stanley, eds. 2007. *Cities of the Middle East and North Africa: A Historical Encyclopedia*. ABC-CLIO/Greenwood.

Harb, Antoine K. 2001. *The Maronites: History and Constants*. The Maronite Heritage Publications.

Harris, William. 2012. *Lebanon: A History, 600–2011*. Oxford University Press.

Herrin, Judith. 1987. *The Formation of Christendom*. Princeton University Press.

Hitti, Philip K. 1951. *History of Syria Including Lebanon and Palestine*. Macmillan.

Hitti, Philip K. 1961. *The Near East in History: A 5000-Year Story*. D. Van Nostrand.

Hitti, Philip K. 1967. *Lebanon in History: From the Earliest Times to the Present*. Macmillan.

Holst, Stanford. 2021. *Phoenicians: Lebanon's Epic Heritage*. Santorini Publishing.

Horsley, Richard A. 1997. *Paul and Empire: Religion and Power in in Roman Empirical Society*. Trinity Press International.

Kelly, John Norman Davidson. 1978. *Early Christian Doctrines*. Harper and Row.

Kaufman, Asher. 2004. *Reviving Phoenicia: The Search for Identity in Lebanon*. I.B. Tauris.

Khalaf, Samir G. 1996. *A Bequest Unearthed, Phoenicia*. Phoenician International Research Center.

Kuhn, Steven L., Mary C. Stiner, David S. Reese, and Erksin Güleç. 2001. *Ornaments of the Earliest Upper Paleolithic: New Insights from the Levant* (Vol. 98). Proceedings of the National Academy of Sciences.

MacCulloch, Diarmaid. 2009. *A History of Christianity: The First Three Thousand Years*. Viking.

Marston, Elsa. 2002. *The Phoenicians - Cultures of the Past*. Marshall Cavendish Corporation.

Mayer, Wendy, and Pauline Allen. 2012. *The Churches of Syrian Antioch (300-638 CE)*. Peeters Publishers.

Meiggs, Russel. 1982. *Trees and Timber in the Ancient Mediterranean*. Clarendon Press.

Mikesell, Marvin W. 1969. "The Deforestation of Mount Lebanon." *The Geographical Review* 59, no. 1 (January): 1-28. Moosa, Matti. 2005. *The Maronites in History*. Gorgias Press.

Moscati, Sabatino. 2001. *The Phoenicians*. I.B. Tauris.

Naaman, Paul. 2011. *The Maronites: The Origins of an Antiochene Church*. Liturgical Press.

Novak, Raymond. M. 2001. *Christianity and the Roman Empire: Background Texts*. Trinity Press.

Phares, Walid. 1979. *Al-Taʿaddudīyah fī Lubnān* [*Pluralism in Lebanon*]. Kaslik University Press.

Quinn, Josephine. C. 2017. *In Search of the Phoenicians*. Princeton University Press.

Rawlinson, George. 2005. *Phoenicia: History of a Civilization*. Longmans, Green, and Co.

Sader, Hélène. 2019. *The History and Archaeology of Phoenicia*. SBL Press.

Skaff, Elias. B. 1993. *The Place of the Patriarchs of Antioch in Church History*. Sophia Press.

Strazzulla, Michela. 2006. *Ancient Lebanon: Monuments Past and Present*. Getty Museum Publications.

von Harnack, Adolf. 1908. *The Mission and Expansion of Christianity in the First Three Centuries,* Vol. 2. Williams and Norgate.

Zalloua, Pierre A., Daniel E. Platt, Mireille El Sibai, Jade Khalife, Nadine Makhoul, Marc Haber, Yali Xue, et al. 2008. "Identifying Genetic Traces of Historical Expansions: Phoenician Footprints in the Mediterranean." *The American Journal of Human Genetics* 83 (5): 633-642. https://doi.org/10.1016/j.ajhg.2008.10.012.

Part Two

Asbridge, Thomas. 2010. *The Crusades: The Authoritative History of the Wars for the Holy Land*. Ecco.

Barber, Malcolm. 2012. *The Crusader States*. Yale University Press.

Bokenkotter, Thomas. 2004. *A Concise History of the Catholic Church*. Doubleday Publishing.

Boor, Karl de, ed. 1883-1885. *Theophanis Chronographia*. 2 vols. Leipzig: B. G. Teubner.

Bury, John B. 1913. *The Cambridge Medieval History*, Vol. 2. Macmillan.

Chadwick, Henry. 2003. *East and West: The Making of a Rift in the Church*. Oxford University Press.

Chasseaud, George. W. 1855. *The Druses of the Lebanon: Their Manners, Customs, and History with a Translation of Their Religious Code*. London: R. Bentley.

Christie, Niall. 2014. *Muslims and Crusaders: Christianity's Wars in the Middle East, 1095–1382*. Routledge.

Collelo, Thomas, ed. 1987. *Lebanon: A Country Study*. Federal Research Division of the Library of Congress.

Dawson, Christopher. 2003. *The Making of Europe: An Introduction to the History of European Unity*. The Catholic University of America Press.

Falk, Avner. 2010. *Franks and Saracens: Reality and Fantasy in the Crusades*. Karnac Books.

Ferguson, Everett. 2005. *Church History, Volume One: From Christ to the Pre-Reformation,* Vol. 1. Zondervan.

Gervers, Michael, and Ramzi J. Bikhazi, eds. 1990. *Conversion and Continuity - Indigenous Christian Communities in Islamic Lands, Eighth to Eighteenth Centuries.* Pontifical Institute of Medieval Studies.

Gregory, Timothy E. 2010. *A History of Byzantium.* Wiley-Blackwell.

Hamilton, Louis. 2025. "Papal Rome in the Middle Ages." In *The Cambridge History of the Papacy*, Vol. 3, *The Papacy*, edited by Joëlle Rollo-Koster, Robert A. Ventresca, Melodie H. Eichbauer, and Miles Pattenden, 35 – 70. Cambridge University Press.

Harpur, James. 2008. *The Crusades: The Two Hundred Years War - The Clash between the Cross and the Crescent in the Middle East 1096-1291.* Rosen Publishing Group.

Heid, Stefan. 2000. *Celibacy in the Early Church - The Beginnings of a Discipline of Obligatory Continence for Clerics in East and West.* Ignatius Press.

Hillenbrand, Carole. 1999. *The Crusades: Islamic Perspectives.* Routledge.

Hitti, Philip K. 1928. *The Origins of the Druze People and Religion.* Columbia University Press.

Holt, Peter M. 1986. *The Age of the Crusades: The Near East from the Eleventh Century to 1517.* Longman.

Irenaeus of Lyons. 1885. *Against Heresies (Adversus Haereses).* Translated by L. Green, edited by M. G. C. P. Vol. 1 of *Ante-Nicene Fathers.* T&T Clark. Reprint, 1985. Christian Classics Ethereal Library.

Kaegi, Walter E. 1995. *Byzantium and the Early Islamic Conquests.* Cambridge University Press.

Kedar, Benjamin Z. 1984. *Crusade and Mission: European Approaches toward the Muslims.* Princeton University Press.

Louth, Andrew. 2007. *Greek East and Latin West: The Church, AD 681–1071.* St. Vladimir's Seminary Press.

Maalouf, Amin. 1984. *The Crusades Through Arab Eyes.* Saqi Books.

McGuckin, John A. 1995. *On the Unity of Christ.* St Vladimirs Seminary Press.

Nicolle, David. 2005. *Yarmuk AD 636: The Muslim Conquest of Syria.* Osprey Publishing.

Nicolle, David. 2011. *The Fourth Crusade 1202-04 - The Betrayal of Byzantium.* Osprey Publishing.

Phares, Walid. 1995. *Lebanese Christian Nationalism: The Rise and Fall of an Ethnic Resistance*: Lynne Rienner Publishers.

Prawer, Joshua. 1989. "Social Classes in the Crusader States: The Minorities." In *The Impact of the Crusades on the Near East*, edited by Norman P. Zacour and Harry W. Hazard, 59–116. Vol. 5 of *A History of the Crusades*, general editor, Kenneth Meyer Setton. University of Wisconsin Press

Qualben, Lars P. 1958. *A History of the Christian Church.* Thomas Nelson.

Rabah, Makram. 2020. *Conflict on Mount Lebanon: The Druze, the Maronites and Collective Memory.* Hurst & Company.

Robinson, Ian S. 2004. *The Papal Reform of the Eleventh Century: Lives of Pope Leo IX and Pope Gregory VII.* Manchester University Press.

Runciman, Steven. 1955. *The Eastern Schism: A Study of the Papacy and the Eastern Churches During the XIth and XIIth Centuries.* Clarendon Press.

Salibi, Kamal S. 1998. *A House of Many Mansions: The History of Lebanon Reconsidered.* I.B. Tauris.

Shelley, Bruce L. 2008. *Church History in Plain Language.* Thomas Nelson.

Sheppard, Jonathan. 2005. *Christendom at the Crossroads: The Medieval Era.* Westminster John Knox Press.

Siecienski, Edward A. 2010. *The Filioque: History of a Doctrinal Controversy.* Oxford University Press.

Ray, Stephen K. 1999. *Upon This Rock: St. Peter and the Primacy of Rome in Scripture and the Early Church.* Ignatius Press.

Valla, Lorenzo. 2007. *On the Donation of Constantine.* Translated by G. W. Bowersock. The I Tatti Renaissance Library. Harvard University Press.

Ware, Timothy. 1993. *The Orthodox Church.* Penguin Books.

Wilken, Robert L. 2003. *The Christians as the Romans Saw Them.* Yale University Press.

Part Three

Abu-Husayn, Abdul-Rahim. 2002. *The View from Istanbul: Ottoman Lebanon and the Druze Emirate.* I.B. Tauris.

Appiah, Kwame A. 2006. *Cosmopolitanism: Ethics in a World of Strangers.* W. W. Norton & Company.

Baily, Samuel L., and Eduardo J. Míguez. 2003. *Mass Migration to Modern Latin America.* Rowman & Littlefield.

Betts, Robert B. 1990. *The Druze.* Yale University Press.

Bayeh, Joseph. 2014. *The Literature of the Lebanese Diaspora: Representations of Place and Transnational Identity.* I.B. Tauris.

Cobban, Helena. 1984. *The Palestinian Liberation Organisation.* Cambridge University Press.

Cohen, Robin. 2008. *Global Diasporas: An Introduction.* Routledge.

El Khazen, Farid. 2000. *The Breakdown of the State in Lebanon, 1967–1976.* Harvard University Press.

Farshee, Louay. 2014. *Safer Barlik: Famine in Mount Lebanon During World War I.* Inkwater Press.

Firro, Kais. 1992. *A History of the Druzes.* E. J. Brill.

Hiro, Dilip. 1993. *Lebanon: Fire and Embers – A History of the Lebanese Civil War.* Palgrave Macmillan.

Hitti, Philip K. 1924. *The Syrians in America.* George H. Doran Company.

Hourani, Albert, and Nadim Shehadi. 1992. *The Lebanese in the World: A Century of Emigration.* I.B. Tauris.

Inglis, Christine. 2006. "On the Beach: Racial Confrontation in Australia." *Migration Information Source*. Web.

Karpat, Kemal H. 1985. "The Ottoman Emigration to America, 1860-1914." *International Journal of Middle East Studies* 17 (2): 175-209.

Katz, Raul L. 2012. *The Impact of Broadband on the Economy: Research to Date and Policy Issues*. ITU Broadband Series. April 2012. International Telecommunication Union (ITU).

Keynes, John M. 1936. *The General Theory of Employment, Interest, and Money*. Harcourt, Brace and Company.

Khalaf, Samir. 2004. *Civil and Uncivil Violence in Lebanon: A History of the Internationalization of Communal Conflict*. Columbia University Press.

Khater, Akram F. 2001. *Inventing Home: Emigration, Gender, and the Middle Class in Lebanon, 1870-1920*. University of California Press.

Lesser, Jeffrey. 1999. *Negotiating National Identity: Immigrants, Minorities, and the Struggle for Ethnicity in Brazil*. Duke University Press.

Makdisi, Ussama. 2000. *The Culture of Sectarianism: Community, History, and Violence in Nineteenth-Century Ottoman Lebanon*. University of California Press.

McCarthy, Justin. 1997. *The Ottoman Turks: An Introductory History to 1923*. Addison Wesley Longman.

Monsour, Andrea. 2005. "Religion Matters: The Experience of Syrian/Lebanese Christians in Australia from the 1880s to 1947." *Humanities Research* 12 (1): 92-106.

Nicolle, David. 2014. *Mamluk 'Askari 1250–1517*. Osprey Publishing.

Palmer, Alan. 1992. *The Decline and Fall of the Ottoman Empire*. Barnes and Noble Books.

Saato, Fred J. 2006. *American Eastern Catholics*. Paulist Press.

Salibi, Kamal S. 1965. *The Modern History of Lebanon*. Weidenfeld & Nicolson.

Salibi, Kamal S. 1976. *Crossroads to Civil War: Lebanon 1958–1976*. Caravan Books.

Salibi, Kamal S. 1998. *A House of Many Mansions: The History of Lebanon Reconsidered*. I.B. Tauris.

Tarazi Fawaz, Leila. 1995. *An Occasion for War: Civil Conflict in Lebanon and Damascus in 1860*. University of California Press.

Traboulsi, Fawwaz. 2007. *A History of Modern Lebanon*. Pluto Press.

Truzzi, Oswaldo. 1997. "The Right Place at the Right Time: Syrians and Lebanese in Brazil and the United States, A Comparative Approach." *Journal of American Ethnic History* 16 (2): 3-34.

Whitehead, Charles. 2010. *Sketch of Antonio Bishallany, a Syrian of Mount Lebanon*. Nabu Press. Originally printed by American Tract Society.

Winslow, Charles. 1996. *Lebanon: War and Politics in a Fragmented Society*. Routledge.

IMAGES CREDIT

The Land of Canaan. Canaanite States in the Bronze Age. Wikimedia Commons. April 20, 2020. Accessed September 14, 2025. Creative Commons Attribution-Share Alike 4.0 International license. https://commons.wikimedia.org/wiki/File:Canaanite_City_States_In_The_Bronze_Age.svg

The Levant. Wikimedia Commons. July 2, 2023. Accessed September 14, 2025. Creative Commons Attribution-Share Alike 4.0 International license. https://commons.wikimedia.org/wiki/File:Levant_(definitions).png

Map of Lebanon. Lebanon Governorates. Wikimedia Commons. May 8, 2023. Accessed September 14, 2025. Creative Commons Attribution-Share Alike 4.0 International license. https://commons.wikimedia.org/wiki/File:Lebanon_governorates_english.svg

Phoenicia. Wikimedia Commons. June 20, 2009. Accessed September 14, 2025. Creative Commons Attribution 3.0 Unported license. https://commons.wikimedia.org/wiki/File:Phoenicia_map-en.svg

The Holy Land. The Historical Geography of the Holy Land, Especially in Relation to the History of Israel and of the Early Church (1897). Wikimedia Commons. October 15, 2015. Accessed September 14, 2025. Flickr's The Commons. https://commons.wikimedia.org/wiki/File:The_historical_geography_of_the_Holy_Land,_especially_in_relation_to_the_history_of_Israel_and_of_the_early_Church_(1897)_(14764303344).jpg

The Great Commission—Travels of St. Paul. Judea and Phenicia. Voyages and Travels of St. Paul - designed and engraved by Thomas Starling (1842). Wikimedia Commons. April 18, 2023. Accessed September 14, 2025. Public Domain. https://commons.wikimedia.org/wiki/File:Judea_and_Phenicia._Voyages_and_Travels_of_St._Paul_-_designed_and_engraved_by_Thomas_Starling..._-_btv1b53119284r_(cropped).jpg

The Five Ecclesiastical Sees (Rome, Constantinople, Alexandria, Antioch, and Jerusalem). Pentarchy 565 CE. Wikimedia Commons. February 21, 2021. Accessed September 14, 2025. Creative Commons Attribution-Share Alike 4.0 International license. https://commons.wikimedia.org/wiki/File:Pentarchy_565_CE.png

Antioch. Principality of Antioch. Wikimedia Commons. July 12, 2010. Accessed September 14, 2025. Creative Commons Attribution 3.0 Unported license. https://commons.wikimedia.org/wiki/File:Principality_of_Antioch_locator.svg

Orontes River from its Source in Lebanon to its Mouth in Türkiye Traversing Northern Syria. Map of the Orontes River. Wikimedia Commons. February 14, 2015. Accessed September 14, 2025. Creative Commons Attribution-Share Alike 4.0 International license. https://commons.wikimedia.org/wiki/File:Map_of_the_Orontes_river.png

The Early Muslim Conquests. Islamic Expansion per caliph. Wikimedia Commons. January 11, 2025. Accessed September 14, 2025. Creative Commons CC0 1.0 Universal Public Domain Dedication. https://commons.wikimedia.org/wiki/File:Islamic_Expansion_per_caliph.png

Author at the Monastery of Saint John Maron, First Patriarchal Residence at Kfarhay. Author photo. July 26, 2025.

Author at the Monastery of Our Lady of Ilige, Patriarchal Residence at Mayfouk. Author photo. July 26, 2025.

The 1054 East-West Schism, Great Schism 1054. Wikimedia Commons. August 28, 2021. Accessed September 14, 2025. GNU Free Documentation License, Version 1.2 (or later). https://commons.wikimedia.org/wiki/File:Great_Schism_1054.svg

The Crusader States. The Crusader States in 1135. Wikimedia Commons. September 8, 2024. Accessed September 14, 2025. Creative Commons Attribution-Share Alike 4.0 International license. https://commons.wikimedia.org/wiki/File:The_Crusader_States_in_1135.svg

Qaim Maqamate Provincial System of Mount Lebanon. The Qaim Maqamiya System Mount Lebanon (1842-1861). Wikimedia Commons. May 21, 2024. Accessed September 14, 2025. Creative Commons Attribution 4.0 International license. https://commons.wikimedia.org/wiki/File:The_Qaim_Maqamiya_System_Mount_Lebanon_(1842-1861).png

Vilayet of Beirut Under the Ottomans. Mount Lebanon, Ottoman Syria 1914. Wikimedia Commons. May 24, 2013. Accessed September 14, 2025. Creative Commons Attribution-Share Alike 3.0 Unported license. https://commons.wikimedia.org/wiki/File:Mount_Lebanon,_Ottoman_Syria_1914.png

Lebanon Distribution of Religious Groups in Lebanon, Lebanese Greek Orthodox Christians Map. Wikimedia Commons. November 22, 2022. Accessed September 14, 2025. Creative Commons Attribution-Share Alike 4.0 International license. https://commons.wikimedia.org/wiki/File:Lebanese_Greek_ Orthodox_Christians_Map.png

Saint Maron's statue on the outer wall of Saint Peter's Basilica, unveiled in 2011 by Pope Benedict XVI. Author Photo. February 23, 2024.

ABOUT THE AUTHOR

Dr. Fadi P. Deek is Distinguished Professor of Informatics and Mathematical Sciences at New Jersey Institute of Technology. He has also served NJIT in a wide range of leadership roles, culminating in Provost and Senior Executive Vice President for a decade and, prior to this, Dean for the College of Science and Liberal Arts, for another decade. Dr. Deek is the author/co-author of five books, 14 book chapters, and 200 scholarly publications in journals and conference proceedings. In addition, he is also the editor/co-editor of five edited collections.

In addition to his commitment to science and technology education and research, he is interested in the evolution of the early Christian Church in Lebanon and the Levant. Above all, Dr. Deek is an activist for peace and prosperity in Lebanon and for all of its citizens.

www.ingramcontent.com/pod-product-compliance
Lightning Source LLC
Chambersburg PA
CBHW020925090426
42736CB00010B/1042